bare hooves
and
open hearts

tales from nelipot cottage

Dear Anne

To Dreams & fun

Jean Marie

xxx

bare hooves
and
open hearts

tales from nelipot cottage

FRAN MCNICOL

Sea Crow Press

nelipot

(n.) one who walks barefoot

pronunciation | **'nel-i-pot**\

This book is dedicated to all the horses who have crossed my path, but most of all to my precious Paddy, for teaching me to ask the right questions.

CONTENTS

FOREWORD

To my good friend Fran... a true horsewoman!

It has taken almost my entire adult lifetime to unlock my young girl passions, those being horses and their welfare. Connecting with such an animal unleashes a person's creativity, individualism and desire to be better.

Meeting Fran and discovering our mutual love for horses will always stand out as a magical moment in my life. I was so excited to connect with someone who had heard the same call to find a better path to equine well-being, someone else who had thought to ask the question "Why do horses wear shoes?"

Equine hooves is how we met — equine hooves and the challenges of attaining a horse's individual barefoot soundness. We stumbled across one another at a hoof care clinic, and we came together in discussion over our shared passion.

Many people have already discovered Fran's musings through her charming online blog, *Nelipot Cottage*. Through stories of her little barefoot herd, she shares her passion for naturalization and natural feeding methods and how she strives to keep her horses holistically happy — with healthy hooves, healthy minds and healthy bodies.

Bare Hooves and Open Hearts presents a collation of Fran's holistic thinking and understandings, her take on horses.

I encourage my fellow equestrians to read these carefully crafted pages and question our modern day practices. Fran's thought-provoking words will intrigue and inspire you. Her goal in sharing these stories is to invite others to join together in manifesting positive energies — in our own lives and in the lives of our horses.

If you are drawn to the charms of natural horse keeping and seeking inspiration to break away from unhealthy traditions, *Bare Hooves and Open Hearts* is the perfect place to start. It tells a vital story based on truths faced and experiences lived, and it deserves to be widely read.

In honest and practical prose, Fran writes about the special bonds, love and admiration she has for her horses. *Bare Hooves and Open Hearts* combines riding memoir, outside the box moments and horse care tips while recounting the joys and woes of everyday life at Nelipot Cottage.

This is the remarkable true story of an authentic horsewoman. We delight in her intimate and poignant stories, her love for her horses and her dog Ernie and the astounding transformations she has experienced.

You took me to adventure and to love. We two have shared great joy and great sorrow. And now I stand at the gate of the paddock watching you run in an ecstasy of freedom, knowing you will return to stand quietly, loyally, beside me. ~ Pam Brown

Emma Bailey
Equine Hoofcare Professional
Liberated Horsemanship Mentor

INTRODUCTION

Nelipot Cottage was first a place — a small house on the outskirts of the Delamere Forest, my dream home, where I planned to live a physically and mentally active life with a husband, three horses and a dog. But it's also the name of an adventure — an adventure that began as an entirely novel equestrian set-up, based on keeping horses in a holistic way, aimed at fulfilling their species-specific needs.

Change, however, is inevitable, and sometimes dreams come true in the strangest of ways. The horses, the dog and I moved away from the physical incarnation of the original Nelipot Cottage, but we take the spirit of it with us. The learning and the journey continue. The Nelipot ethos endures, and its focus is on the optimal care of the modern sports and leisure horse. We aim to cultivate healthy hooves, healthy bodies and, most of all, a healthy mind.

Healthy Hooves.

My horses may be happy and healthy and covered in mud most of the time, but I also condition them to work. We enjoy drag hunting and eventing and have covered many miles around our beautiful forest. Keeping my horses barefoot, without steel horseshoes, is a foundational part of my philosophy.

As I learn more, I find it increasingly clear that metal horseshoes are a modern convenience, really only required in order to compensate for deficiencies in our contemporary animal husbandry practices. Nailing on steel shoes actually appears to damage the hoof and can even shorten the horse's life. To me, the price of convenience is not acceptable. I operate on the idea that barefoot, ethical horse management is completely compatible with having fit, quality horses who can compete and work hard and thrive in any discipline.

Healthy Bodies.

Another key element of the Nelipot philosophy is natural horse husbandry. Horses have three species-specific needs — friends, forage and freedom. My horses are turned out as much as possible. At Nelipot they were living as a small, settled bachelor herd with plenty of room to move around and access to ad lib forage. In this way, we meet all their physical and social needs. The living out is also a great labour-saving strategy!

Domestication is surprisingly difficult for horses. We humans tolerate a range of stereotypical stress behaviours in our horses, such as weaving and crib-biting, which we would find distressing if we saw them in a zoo animal. But somehow, many of us have fooled ourselves into normalising and managing these behaviours in the domesticated horse.

These stereotypical behaviours are often the result of physical ailments such as gastric ulcers — incredibly prevalent in both performance horses and leisure horses — and a key indicator of the stress that many domesticated horses live under. I take them as a flashing sign that traditional horse management practices are not keeping our adored horses healthy or happy.

Rather than not keeping horses at all, or simply accepting that we must compromise their needs and deal with the resulting health issues, perhaps we could learn to keep horses in a way that promotes their health in the best way we can. It seems to me a small thank you for the generosity with which they allow us to share their immense power and grace.

Healthy Minds.

Many competition horses, even at the lower levels, are fairly obviously stressed and unhappy in their work, as well as in their downtime. Training should, ideally, enhance our relationship with our horses, making the partnership itself a beautiful exchange between horse and human. Classical training should also enhance the body, empowering the horses and preparing them physically for a long and healthy ridden career.

It was many years before I found a trainer who could teach me how to improve my horses' body and mind, not just sit on them and go through the motions. I'm hoping that the horse lovers and riders who read this book will get a better sense of what is possible, and go seeking the few true masters left in the world before it is too late, before that precious knowledge dies with them.

Training a horse is an intellectual as well as a physical activity — healthy minds are essential for the humans in the partnership. Learning to care for our horses better will turn us into better humans. And the world certainly needs more of those!

The Team.

The four-legged Nelipot team consists of Paddy, Cal, Rocky, and Ernie the Dog.

Paddy was the original barefoot convert. He is a dark bay, mostly thoroughbred Irish Sport Horse, now retired at the grand age of twenty-four. Paddy is the horse who started me on my great barefoot journey; he is responsible for all the accelerated learning that ensued. Without Paddy, there would have been no barefoot epiphany, no journey of discovery, and no Nelipot stories to tell.

He has been a patient and tolerant teacher, and this book is dedicated to him.

His main job nowadays is that of herd lookout. He has to know where each horse is at all times, and he will always sense me coming and greet me with a periscope neck, full-on gaze and pointed ears when I am walking the dog or doing late-night checks in the evening.

Cal is a fifteen-year-old Irish Sport Horse: half Irish Draft, half thoroughbred. He somehow got more of the heavy horse blood than the finer thoroughbred, so he is a very impressive war horse now that he is advanced in his work and has developed all his muscles.

He started off dark bay as a youngster, went through an interesting pink roan phase, had a few smart dappled grey years, and is now really quite pale, working his way through to snowy white. He is fabulously bold across country and a great fun and safe all-rounder.

Rocky is my posh warmblood — bright bay with a small white star, just turned eight and still quite gangly. I bought him as a yearling and his early life and training have been quite an odyssey. You will find several chapters in this book that tell the stories of his trials and tribulations.

Ernie is a liver brown German Short-Haired Pointer. He's five now, and the best dog that any human could wish for. His great gift is simply to bring love and joy to every day. I think that all humans should have the opportunity to be adored by a dog at least once in their life.

1

BARE HOOVES ARE BEST

On the day that would become the defining moment of my equestrian evolution, I was nowhere near the stables.

I was at work, as I often was in my busy life as a junior doctor, and I had organised for my beloved horse Paddy to get sorted with a shiny new set of steel horseshoes for the last important competition of the season.

I can't remember what I was doing when the telephone rang, but I do recall the farrier sounding fairly sheepish. As well he might. He had managed to remove all the old, worn out horseshoes, but Paddy was simply not allowing him to nail the new shoes on.

I had first contacted this particular farrier about shoeing Paddy because our regular guy had essentially sacked us. I did explain to him that this horse was very tricky to shoe, and he had told me not to worry. He even professed to be a bit of a horse whisperer.

As he recounted to me over the phone, in great detail, how Paddy had fretted and stressed and finally flung him clean across the yard, I came to understand that the whispering must have stopped a while ago.

Paddy was the first horse I bought of my very own. He arrived in my life when I was thirty-two, the childhood dream finally came true. He was sixteen-one hands high, mostly thoroughbred, long-legged, and fine-boned. He was, and still is, very handsome, jet black without a speck of white on him, and a lovely elegant mover. All in all, he was a perfect lady's horse. He was a real life Black Beauty, a wish finally granted for the pony-mad child still hiding under my serious doctor exterior.

He was relatively cheap, due to a fearsome reputation as an unhappy and troubled horse. He came from a professional eventing yard, and the first story was that he needed to be caught in the stable to be saddled up. Apparently, if you showed him the saddle first before tying him up he would run around the stable, pointing his bum at you to avoid being caught.

He didn't much like being groomed. He hated the vet, hated being wormed and, most of all, he hated the farrier.

The guy who sold him to me told me all about his quirks and said that, in his opinion, Paddy would do better as a much-loved single horse belonging to a devoted amateur rider who would fuss over him, and build a bond with him, and who had the time and patience to deal with his idiosyncrasies.

And do you know what? As time would tell, he was broadly right. But then work got too busy and I couldn't keep Paddy fit without help. I sent him on polo livery, because the daily exercise required to keep him at full eventing fitness was included in the substantial livery price.

Paddy settled in well and was happy there, until his favourite groom left and was replaced by a young German girl with a very authoritarian approach to horse management. Reading between the lines, I worked out that Ms Munich and the Whispering Smith had been struggling with escalating anxiety from the horse for some time. When the established tactic of bribery with food had failed, they tried Sedalin, an oral sedative medicine, along with increasing levels of pressure.

It had apparently been getting more and more difficult to complete the shoeing, but it wasn't until the total failure occurred that Ms Munich saw fit to tell me they were having problems. I suppose that part of the substantial fee I was paying was to make sure I didn't get bothered with the tiresome daily details of looking after a horse.

So there they were, at opposite ends of the yard — the big black horse with no shoes on, and the supposedly horse-whispering smith with his dignity in tatters. You simply cannot go head to head and win a fight with this horse. You never really win a fight with any horse, of course, but Paddy is much more likely to actually fight back than submit to fear and give in. The embarrassed farrier told me that my horse would have to be formally sedated by the vet before he could even think of getting the shoes back on. I gulped, sighed, and said yes.

'Please organise that as soon as possible,' I said. 'I'm competing the next two Sundays.'

One Day Eventing involves three phases of competition: dressage on grass, show-jumping a course of coloured poles that will fall down if tapped, also on grass, and finally the cross country phase, galloping up hill and down dale, jumping solid, natural-looking obstacles. I *needed* Paddy to have those shoes.

So we got the vet out, formally sedated my horse, and successfully hot-shod him so I could compete in the last events of the season. That set of shoes came in at around £150, what with the added cost of the vet's visit and the drugs. I had known polo ponies and other high-level competition horses that needed to be sedated when shod, and I knew owners who just accepted that as normal, the cost of doing business. But I didn't have that kind of budget. I'm ashamed to say that the main problem for me at the time was that £150 every six weeks was a punitive price.

Whatever the motivation, it did start me thinking. Furiously, as my brain whirled round and round, I kept asking myself — Is there another way?

Traditionally, horses wear steel horseshoes, unless they are not in work and officially don't need them. I could remember little ponies at riding school with no shoes and, later, my German sister's Arab horse regularly doing thirty mile rides through her local forest without shoes. In fact, there were quite a few horses without shoes in that village in Germany, doing lots of work and looking very well.

But they were all Arabian horses or other breeds known for their endurance, or German ponies famed for their hardiness. I live in Britain, and I had always wanted to go eventing, and anyone in the British eventing scene will tell you that horses need studs to do cross country safely. So my horse clearly did need his shoes. Of course he did.

Paddy's hooves were weak. They looked terrible, the horn was crumbly, the feet barely holding the nails needed to keep the shoes on. We had so much trouble that we were down to a five week shoeing cycle. I started to ask myself: what if he could actually do without shoes? Could I do other riding without studs? Was there a way I could event him without using studs at all? Did I really need to event him? Could I find him another job? Did I need to sell him if he couldn't do the work I wanted him to do?

Paddy had been quite cheap to buy because he came with a horrible reputation. Part of that reputation was that he was notoriously bad to shoe. There are two ways of fitting horseshoes. Cold shoeing involves nailing prefabricated steel shoes onto the horse's hoof. Farriers carry a selection of shoes of various sizes in their vans. With hot shoeing, the shoes are heated in a forge and reshaped on an anvil, so they can be tweaked to fit the horse. The stud holes are tapped in at that stage.

When I first got Paddy, we managed to cold shoe him relatively easily, with a bucket of feed at the top end to keep him occupied. However, once I started eventing with him, I went with the conventional wisdom which said he needed studs to help him grip during the cross country phase. So we moved to hot shoeing, and the problems with the farrier escalated.

Fortuitously, I had a climbing acquaintance who was married to a barefoot trimmer. A vaguely remembered conversation at a summer party got me thinking back to the barefoot horses I had known in Germany, all of them managing perfectly well without shoes, hacking and jumping and galloping. I started reading. I started asking lots of questions, re-examined what I knew about shoes and horses, spoke to the trimmer girl at length, changed Paddy's diet on her advice, started buying powdered magnesium oxide by the kilo and, six weeks later, at the end of the eventing season, we pulled my horse's shoes off for the last time.

He was twelve years old.

Paddy was lame on stones at first, as you would be if I took your shoes off and sent you running down a gravel drive, but luckily the polo yard was in a rural area surrounded by roads and lanes of super-smooth tarmac. Suddenly, with no skidding metal horseshoes, all those steep, narrow country roads felt much safer to ride on. There was a local common with a sand track to canter laps on, so Paddy never missed any work. He would tiptoe down the gravel drive, zoom down the smooth tarmac and pull like a train around the common. After about two months, he zoomed down the gravel drive too, then down the hard core. Paddy zooms everywhere!

We started jumping again, with initial trepidation on my part because of the lack of shoes, but he actually felt better — he adjusted his balance automatically and stopped rushing his fences. Grip just didn't seem to be an issue.

His feet got stronger and stronger.

He went on to have a couple of amazing seasons eventing. We

got to the Riding Club National Championships for One Day Eventing, as well as for Hunter Trials (this involves just the cross country, the fun bit), and we moved up to BE100, the third level of affiliated competition. He was never the most consistent horse, but he became a cross country superstar on his good days.

In retrospect, it was all so obvious: the hatred of the farrier was purely a pain reaction from thin soles; the poor hoof quality was due to poor nutrition (even though we used a reputable and popular feed brand, in nice shiny packaging), and from the damage caused by repetitive hot shoeing.

From once having the worst feet in Cheshire, Paddy now has the best, toughest, most functional feet you could wish for.

That day, when the call from the farrier came, was the defining moment of my horsemanship career, because that was the day I first chose to question dogma and tradition. Even more importantly, the choice I made — to take Paddy's shoes off and try him barefoot — was a choice that put my horse's needs before my own aspirations.

I listened to what my horse was telling me. I relinquished my agenda for the health of my horse. In doing so, I chose the road less travelled. On the day I made that decision, my relationship with Paddy, my relationship with all my future horses, changed completely.

In law, horses are chattels, possessions, to be bought and sold. They exist to do a job. There is no recognition under the law of the land, or even very much in equine science, that these magnificent animals might be sentient beings, creatures who could be perfectly capable of communicating with us if we could only take the time to listen.

Once you start listening, once you offer that animal a voice, an opinion, a say in the relationship, then the bond you will forge is like no other. The rewards are beyond number.

Dogs love you unconditionally and always want to be with

you, no matter how uncertain you are. Horses will choose, if they are allowed to and not coerced into compliance. They insist on congruence, on peaceful, calm thoughts, on loving intent. Those moments of calm, of shared breath, of touch — forehead to forehead — become unutterably precious. Paddy is still my most loved horse; nothing like a possession, but a friend beyond price.

Although Paddy did force my hand, I stepped into our new choice and embraced it with an open mind. There are many humans in similar situations who have made a different choice, ignored their horse's clear message, persevered with sedation, and then had to move on to remedial shoeing as the foot weakened even further.

The farrier and the vet both told me that Paddy would never cope without shoes, that he would break down in six months, that I was mad for even trying to take him barefoot. His front feet have never been a neat pair, and they told me he would need constant expert attention to ensure his hooves were symmetrical and that he stayed fit and functional. It is a scary and lonely feeling, especially for a well-educated and thoroughly brainwashed young doctor, to go against the advice of the scientific expert. My heart was in my mouth and my breathing shallow with doubt when I waved the farrier off for the last time.

When I bought Paddy, I was on a great livery yard with a crowd of really good friends. We had all bought horses of a similar age at around the same time. Paddy turned out to be the soundest and longest working of all the horses from those days. In the end, I retired him to protect him from the excessive expectations of my now ex-husband: Paddy's body was growing stiff with age, but he would never stop marching out. Even now, he looks at me as if to say, Let's just go galloping!

For him, braving the transition to bare hooves really was the best solution.

A few years ago, Paddy, by then a twenty-year-old barefoot

machine, went charging around the hills above Colwyn Bay on a fun ride with the Flint and Denbigh. We had a great day. He galloped up the hills, trotted up the steep lanes, jumped most things and kept right up with the thrusters. However, the reason the old boy got dragged up the hill that day was because Cal, currently my main horse, is not quite such a barefoot legend. Cal had bruised his soles on Boxing Day racing around Rivington Pike on really stony paths with the Holcombe Harriers. Paddy would have been fine up there, but for Cal it was all a bit too much and he was still pretty footsore a few days later.

Why is Cal not a rock-crunching barefoot horse like Paddy? The painful lessons I have learned as I labour to answer that question form much of the basis of this book. My sincere hope is that others can learn from my experience.

Pause for thought:

- Is there anything you do to your horse that he/she really hates?
- What might they be trying to tell you?
- Is there a way of eliminating the hated thing from their life?

2

BRAVING BAREFOOT — THE GOOD, THE BAD AND THE UGLY

Every time I make a new horsey friend who doesn't know and understand why I am such a keen advocate for keeping my horses barefoot, I find myself re-telling the story that has got me and my horses to this point. And that story covers every aspect of the good, the bad and the ugly of keeping a hard-working horse without shoes.

The Good.

The best thing — and I mean simply the best thing — about keeping ridden horses barefoot, and eventing barefoot horses, is never having to worry about using studs ever again. In the UK, many competition riders screw metal studs into their horse's shoes to increase the foot's grip in the mud for jumping or galloping cross country. By not having the shoes to screw studs into, I eliminate hours of stress and prep: the cleaning out of stud holes, tapping stud holes, packing stud holes, putting in studs, searching for studs in the long grass, chasing the hopping foot around with the tap still in the hole, and all the other nightmares associated with screwing studs into the shoes that are attached to a very excited horse that can't wait to get out on the cross country course.

I don't have to worry about what size of stud to use, nor do I have to suffer the possible damage done to foot and forelimb by the unnatural stress and shear force transmitted to the horse's leg from a studded foot.

You know how footballers are always fracturing their tarsal bones? This is often due to the studded football boot gripping suddenly at speed and all that kinetic energy getting transmitted to the bones of the foot at an angle and intensity that those bones are not meant to withstand. Horses' feet are meant to flex, in order to absorb the concussion of landing, and are also designed to slide a little before gripping, to protect the bones and ligaments of the foot and the even more precious bones and tendons above.

Without shoes and studs, the horse's foot can do just that. Without shoes and studs, we get the benefit of the horse's natural gripping mechanism. The equine hoof is beautifully designed to function on all surfaces when healthy. A concave sole with a pointed toe allows the foot to dig in for extra lift. The fully developed spongy frog at the back of the hoof provides grip, slows the sliding and acts as a cushion shock absorber, a bit like Nike Airs, that also helps to pump blood back up the limb. The bars and quarters act like the cleats in a pair of football boots.

Keeping the ridden horse barefoot also ensures that the horse benefits from optimal proprioception, especially important when we subject them to an unpredictable and sometimes less than perfectly balanced human load. Proprioception is the perception of awareness of the position and movement of the body, and is a key component of the information required for the horse, or any animal, to move well. Put simply, it is the ability to feel the ground beneath their feet. The ability to access and use that information in order to adjust to uneven or challenging terrain is a vital part of balance and of healthy movement, for human or horse. Our day to day human shoes are mostly supple and flex with our feet; metal horseshoes simply do not.

I often think that being shod with steel shoes must feel like being permanently stuck in winter mountaineering boots with crampons. Winter boots, like ski boots, have a completely rigid sole that does not flex at all, although they do allow more ankle bend. Can you imagine trying to walk any distance in your ski boots? You have to do the funky chicken in the joints above to make up for the fact the foot doesn't flex as it was meant to. Can you remember how cold your feet get in ski boots, or even in wellies, in winter? That feeling when your feet are like blocks of ice, solid lumps with no fine touch sensation, and it's difficult to wriggle your toes? And you feel like you are walking on chunks of solid flesh rather than a fully functioning foot? That feeling is even worse when the metal from the crampons conducts the cold through to the sole of the foot.

That loss of feeling is caused by decreased blood circulation; in the cold the blood flow to our extremities is reduced to prevent us losing excessive heat from those areas. The foot goes cold, and numb, and is less functional.

Thermal imaging allows us to compare the temperature difference, and therefore blood flow, between a shod foot and a barefoot hoof. Immobility or inflexibility leads to impaired circulation. When your feet are cold you wiggle your toes to get the blood going; likewise a functioning equid foot flexes and contracts as it lands on the ground, pushing the blood around the hoof and limb. The horn is still a living substance, more solid than our foot but certainly not as rigid as we are led to believe. Overly tight shoes also lead to impaired circulation. We know this from our own experience; why would horses be different?

What do steel horseshoes do? The rigidity of the steel limits the natural flexibility of the foot, converting an adaptable, dynamic structure into a fixed, immobilised structure. The nails and the tightness of the shoe interfere with blood circulation. Even if the shoes are beautifully fitted to the hoof on day one of the shoeing cycle, as the hoof grows, the shoe and the nails become restrictive. Just observe how quickly the hoof grows while the horse is out of shoes during the recommended winter shoeing break. Compare this to the retarded growth you get in between shoeing cycles.

The reduced circulation from restrictive shoeing mimics chilled toes; the horse therefore suffers from decreased proprioception, both from cold feet and from being deprived of crucial mechanical contact between the sole of the foot and the ground. In a healthy equine foot, the sponge like frogs at the heel of the hoof act as extra pumps, moving blood around the foot and back up the limb, and the network of tiny blood vessels within the substance of the hoof act as a hydrostatic (fluid) shock absorption mechanism.

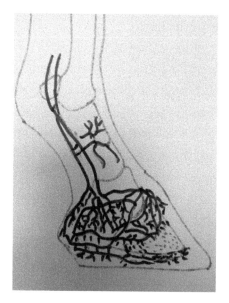

Hoof Blood Supply

We could say that the unshod horse has five hearts pushing the blood around the body, the heart and the four frogs. A cadaver (frozen tissue) model has actually shown that a barefoot hoof absorbs nearly all the concussion created by landing the limb, and therefore very little force is transmitted further up the leg. This shock absorption in the hooves minimises the wear and tear on the rest of the joints above.

Another interesting fact is that steel horseshoes vibrate at the exact same frequency that causes the work-acquired injury known as vibration white finger in humans using industrial power tools. It's a frequency that causes necrosis, also known as tissue death. Not all horseshoes do this — Cytek and other plastic shoes don't have this effect, nor do aluminium racing plates. But steel horseshoes do.

The Bad.

What are the disadvantages of keeping ridden horses barefoot? The main problem that I have observed is that we get instant, accurate feedback about how fit, well and sound (or otherwise) our horses are. But this isn't a disadvantage, I hear you cry!

Not all feedback is welcome or positive, depending on your point of view.

A horse that is sound only in shoes is not truly sound.

That truth is not an easy motto to live by, but it is the truth. Keeping ridden horses barefoot gives us daily, reliable information about our horses' fitness for the work of the day. Lucinda Green, one of our most famous British eventers, tells a great story about a racing trainer who has recently started doing the early season steady conditioning work with all his horses barefoot. He is noticing fewer injuries in the early season, and much better longevity from his charges. Why? Because shoeing had previously allowed him to work the horses harder than their bones, joints and tendons were ready for. By building up the work but keeping the horses barefoot, he could only increase the intensity of work at the rate that the feet were conditioned for, which accurately reflected the conditioning of the limbs above.

When keeping the ridden horse barefoot, we also get instant feedback about our horse's general health. Event lines are ridges that appear in the horn of the hoof and document times of metabolic challenge. Like rings in a tree, or ridges in your fingernails, an event line appears for each dose of wormer, each vaccination, every flush of grass. If you've moved yards, or if your horse has had an injury, or gone through any period of stress, there will be a ripple visible.

Is your horse foot-sore on stones, once the initial barefoot transition period is over? Mostly this means too much sugar in its diet, or that there is another pro-inflammatory process going on. I am now ashamed that it took me a good few years of looking at hundreds of pictures of hooves to twig that Cal's funny-looking slipper feet were actually the feet of a borderline laminitic.

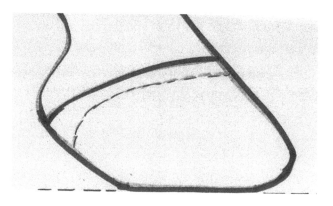

Poor Hoof

Laminitis is a funny disease — like human diabetes, the main cause is a disordered sugar metabolism that affects the whole body. It is not just a disease limited to the equine foot. The horse's hoof is the end organ most often damaged by the disease, like diabetic foot injuries in humans. Cal had terrible airway inflammation, low level laminitic feet, probable stomach ulcers and some very peculiar skin lumps. All of these were manifestations of systemic (whole body) inflammation. Once I listened to the story his feet were telling me and addressed the underlying inflammation, I found the answer to all of his ailments. The solution was a strictly organic, low sugar, low starch diet, with wrapped late cut meadow hay and scientifically-researched organic plant-based supplements for hindgut health and maximum anti-oxidant support. All of this helped his digestive system to work at its peak efficiency.

So, the main disadvantage of keeping the ridden horse barefoot is that you will inevitably become much more in tune with your horse's body. Once you start listening and observing, I warn you now, not all that information is welcome. You may have to adjust your plans and ambitions to fit in with the horse's schedule, with their current capabilities. Your ego may have to step aside, you may have to withdraw from a planned competition. Your training may have to proceed according to the horse's rate of fitness, rather than the eventing calendar, or qualification for the winter dressage championships. You may have to learn new skills, such as a little light hoof trimming. You may have to become a feed geek, or a grass geek, or even get a whole degree's worth of knowledge from bitter experience. It's a lot to take in. But I say it's worth it.

The Ugly.

My vet friend said to me many years ago — You do see some really odd-shaped feet on barefoot horses. He said this as if it were a problem, as if the trimming was at fault, or those misshapen hooves were dangerous to the horse's long-term soundness. He was most offended by lack of symmetry, and that someone could allow it to persist.

My current level of understanding is that feet reflect both what's going on inside the horse and also above the hoof in the rest of the musculoskeletal system. If the horse has funny-looking feet, it's likely because it needs those funny looking feet or because, at this moment, it can only grow funny looking feet. Fix the diet, treat the whole horse, allow and correct the movement, and beautiful feet will grow. Simple but not easy.

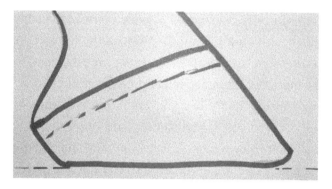

Ideal Hoof

Asking How? and Why? of any horse-care professional is your right and your duty as guardian of your horse. If you are not yet ready to not shoe, then do please give the horse and those precious feet a good long break from shoes every year, to preserve your horse's longevity. We have known since Victorian times that the dreaded navicular is a disease seen almost exclusively in the shod horse. Back-to-back shoeing, a new set every 4-6 weeks, with never a break, is bad for hooves.

Educate yourself. Turn into a hoof geek. And a horse health geek. Ask questions. Be honest with yourself — what do you see when you look at your horse's feet?

And remember the old, wise saying: no foot, no horse.

Further Reading;

Braithwaite, Sarah, and Barker, Nick, *Feet First: Barefoot Performance and Hoof Rehabilitation* Trafalgar Square Books (2009)

3

THE FIRST STEP: DIET

The first step to keeping your ridden horse barefoot, successfully, at a high level of performance, has nothing to do with taking the shoes off. When you transition to barefoot from shod, the first step is to clean up the diet. If your horse is not performing as well as he could barefoot, your top priority should be to go back and examine the diet. Success in barefoot performance or barefoot rehabilitation is determined by four factors: diet, environment, exercise and trim. Those well-meaning naysayers who fail at the barefoot experiment have invariably just taken the horse's shoes off and expected instant success, without taking the first step and making crucial husbandry and lifestyle changes.

I have no formal equine nutritional qualifications. But I am a doctor, specialising in colorectal disease, and my MD research was on inflammation and sepsis. I know a huge amount about inflammation and the gut, and I can critically appraise mammalian as well as human research and then work out which worthwhile theory to apply to my own life.

The horse should eat a forage-based diet. Equids are trickle feeders; in the wild they will browse, forage and graze for sixteen hours a day. However, a forage-based diet doesn't mean they should be standing in a lush green paddock of ryegrass, stuffing their faces, or being surrounded by free choice ad lib ryegrass hay. When we look at photos of wild horse country around the world, we may observe that at most times of the year there is not a blade of green grass to be seen. Trickle feeding a forage based diet means the horses should have to work quite hard for their forage, but also that it should be available more or less non-stop. Unless you are going to drive around the horses' field all day dispensing wedges of different forage at regular intervals, for true species-specific husbandry you have to get quite creative. Track systems encourage natural movement. But the grass on track systems tends to get stressed, so the horses should have free access to other stuff, hay or haylage, trees and natural hedgerows, well stocked with a variety of weeds, and herbs.

Cal, my grey horse, has had breathing problems in the past, so I feed organic, late cut, meadow haylage that is more like wrapped hay. Haylage is cut grass, wrapped when damp, which then ferments, so it has very few viable moulds or spores compared to hay. Forage has to be organic. I found that out the hard way. Fertiliser residue in forage causes all sorts of strange toxic effects. When we first moved to our new field, we bought gorgeous looking meadow hay off the farmer next door. It smelt lovely, tested fine for sugar and starch, and was available in the right quantity at the right price. But the horses just didn't look quite right on it. Their coats were poor, their muscle tight and stringy, and they were thin despite an ad lib feeding system. We switched to organic forage and they bloomed.

I also believe that everything we feed horses should be non-GMO. This should probably apply to everything we humans eat too, but most animal owners will know that the animals get looked after much better than the humans! I know that some genetic

modification does occur every time we breed an animal, or cultivate a plant, but ambitious humans have mostly used GMO technology to increase plants' resistance to chemicals so that they can
then use ever more toxic poisons on the crop to increase yield. So
organic, nitrate free, glyphosate free and non-GMO are unlikely to
occur in the same space.

Round-up is the commonest glyphosate. Glyphosate is an
herbicide. It is applied to the leaves of plants to kill both broadleaf
plants and grasses. The sodium salt form of glyphosate is used to
regulate plant growth and ripen fruit. Glyphosate was first regis-
tered for use in the U.S. in 1974. Glyphosate is used as a desic-
cant: if it is applied to wheat just before harvest, the wheat dies by
going to seed, thereby increasing the yield from the harvest.

Let that sink in for a moment. The wheat dies. Would you like
your horse to eat cereal that had been sprayed with poisonous
weedkiller to kill it just before it has been harvested? And what
about you?

The rest of the barefoot horse's diet, once you get your forage
right, is relatively easy. They shouldn't need much else. If your
forage is good quality and they have varied grazing with access to a
variety of herbs and weeds, they really shouldn't need much else. I
say that with my tongue in my cheek. Rewilding is a relatively new
name for an ancient concept — living in harmony and balance
with nature. The story of Knepp, in Julia Tree's beautifully
written book, is a recent high profile example of this concept in
action. It took me three years of hard work to get my supposedly
horse-friendly grass field in Cheshire up to a paltry eight different
species per square metre. (There will be more to follow regarding
plant diversity in subsequent chapters).

It was a lightbulb moment for me when I realised that my
main crop is not grass, but horses. If your field, like most of
Cheshire, has only one or two plant species per metre, then you
may need to supplement the horses' diet with vitamins and miner-

als. The carrier feed for the supplement should be organic, non-GMO, low sugar, and low starch. I would suggest feeding straights, so that you know exactly what you are feeding. If you must feed processed feed in nice shiny bags, then be sure to avoid anything that contains oatmeal or wheatmeal (industrial floor sweepings), soya oil or meal, (the balance of omega 3/6/9 is completely wrong and actually predisposes to inflammation), and molasses flavouring. Read your labels. And don't believe marketing ploys like the Laminitis Trust badge or friendly sounding names like Healthy Hooves. Read the labels again and do your own research.

Avoid overfeeding. Fat predisposes to insulin resistance, and also has a pro-inflammatory effect on the body. In humans, obesity is a strong independent predictor for cancer, diabetes and heart problems, because fat itself excretes damaging inflammatory-signalling chemicals called cytokines.

In terms of the mineral supplement content, magnesium oxide is really useful in the early transition days. Magnesium is deficient in most Western soils and diets. Horses and humans rarely test deficient in magnesium because both blood and serum levels are very tightly regulated, but supplementing it has been shown anecdotally and experimentally to have positive effects, for health and well- being, as well as for barefoot transition. Magnesium also has an analgesic (painkilling) effect, for which we now use it routinely during human surgery. This analgesic effect helps horses to step out and use their hooves better in the early stages of barefoot adaptation. Salt is crucial, as are copper and zinc, to balance out the excess iron in our British soils. I feed a 25ml scoop of table salt every day, and more in summer if they are working hard. If you can buy sea salt by the 25kg bag that's probably better for them, but I've chosen ease over quality here.

There are many good all-round feed balancers on the market to ease the transition from previously shod to fully functioning barefoot riding horse. If you live in the UK, I would go with a

British barefoot brand; these people have done their homework, their horses have travelled the miles, and they have developed a product based on the needs of the barefoot equine that they have identified from their own experience. A barefoot horse will tell you categorically if the husbandry is good enough, by developing rock crunching high mileage hooves.

So there you have it; the first step to taking the ridden horse barefoot is to forensically examine and perhaps change what you feed. Good hard-working feet rely on good, clean, healthy nutrition, and it's important to set yourself up for success with this crucial first step.

Most of this advice would serve us humans well too. Horses first though.

4

HOW MUCH GRASS DO HORSES NEED?

I have been lucky enough to spend some time in Mongolia, the original land of the horse. In 2018, I volunteered to be one of two doctors on a scientific expedition to the Altai mountains in the west of Outer Mongolia. Horses were our main form of transport, and our expedition team included a zoologist, a botanist, and an archeologist, as well as the herdsman who looked after us and our trusty steeds. Amongst the many lessons came the opportunity to learn from the botanist and the herdsmen about the incredibly bio-diverse plants of Mongolia, in the context of fodder and medicine for the sturdy little mountain horses.

When you look out across the steppes, mountains and plains of Western Mongolia, it all looks really green. However, when you get closer to the green, standing on the ground or sitting on your horse, it's actually sandy, rocky, shaley soil, with a patchy smattering of plants, mostly succulents. The western moun-tainous part of the country is very arid, with little ground mois-ture, so succulents and hardy herbs and weeds do best. The plants were often tiny, yet with really complex, swollen, tuber-like root systems. Trees were a rarity, growing only in sheltered ravines or by oases or rivers. Winter had been late that year, so the flowers weren't really out when we arrived, but they did start to appear later in the trip when there had been some rain. We flew into and out of Khovd, the small domestic airport that serves Western Mongolia, and we could see a definite difference in the green cover between arriving and leaving, two weeks apart.

The horses were tough little buggers, approximately 13-14hh. They were all barefooted, obviously. None of the horses are trained to pick their feet up and none of the herdsman owned a rasp, so not only are they not shod, they are never trimmed by human hand either. Feet varied in shape, although the majority were very similar to the optimum hoof we see in the books on American mustangs by Pete Ramey and Jaime Jackson: there were some hooves with flares, and others with slightly longer toes. The feet were all incredibly tough and highly functional.

We travelled across boulder fields, up and down stony mountain tracks, across steep scree slopes, as well as across the green(ish) foothills and the more gravelly steppes, and the little horses picked their way confidently over all terrain, for twenty to thirty kilometres a day, and were still keen to charge into camp at the end of their long journey.

We would give them a day off after a few tough days, and they had a very easy last day which the herdsman cursed us for: it took them two hours to round them all up for their night-time trip back over the hills for their next clients. Even in hobbles, some of the ponies could move pretty fast! They were lean, but very fit. They got a snack at lunchtime, grazing around in hobbles while we ate our little picnic boxes of pasta or cracked wheat with chewy beef, and they were careful to drink copiously from every stream we crossed. At night, the bits were slipped from their mouths, although the rawhide bridles were left on, and they were hobbled and turned loose around the campsite. In the morning the herdsman would jump on the nearest horse and go and round up the others, ready for action.

There are over three thousand plant species described in Mongolia, with over nine hundred and seventy-five having a use in traditional medicine. On the lower slopes of the Altai mountains, our botanist told us, we should expect to find fourteen to eighteen different species of plant within a metre square. None of these are species that you and I would recognise as grass. There were lots of varieties from the pea family, a Mongolian thistle, Mongolian chives (delicious as a snack when travelling), bellflowers, Iris, Ephedra, and Artemesia or wormseed. My olfactory memory of our trip will be a perfume made up of Artemesia, DEET insecticide, leather and horse sweat — a heady combination indeed!

There wasn't much grass at all in the high mountain country. The herdsman and the botanist knew which plants contained the minerals and vitamins the animals needed for good health, and the horses self-selected crucial snacks at every opportunity. At stream crossings, while waiting their turn, they took the chance to grab mouthfuls of the more lush reeds and grasses. If we stopped to take photographs of a new variety of herb or plant, the horses also checked out what we had found and had a quick munch.

In Hustain, back in the east and south of Ulan Bataar, there is a reserve where the Przewalski horses thrive in the wild. Here, at lower altitudes, the plains were greener and lusher, and we counted eighteen to twenty-five species within a square metre, and over ninety varieties of plant just in the small valley where our campsite was situated.

There were more varied grasses here, as well as numerous wildflowers and herbs. The Takhi, or Przewalski, were very plump when we met them, but they get a very short summer and a long harsh winter, so presumably they were layering up fat for the cold. None of them seemed to have diseased or sore feet.

Back home on the edge of our forest, I looked at a few scattered metre squares in my field. I got up to nine species of plant in the best one, and had about twenty species of plants altogether if I counted the hedgerows and the low hanging tree branches. I was delighted to find Prunella Vulgaris or Selfheal. What a useful weed! I managed to collect a varied bouquet of grass flowers from our rewilding area, over-seeded with gifts from a consultant friend who had inadvertently bought one of the last remaining areas of upland hay meadow in the UK with his retirement cottage on Anglesey.

So, how much grass do horses need? The answer seems to be not much grass at all actually. As long as they have access to a wide variety of plants including some grasses, herbs, weeds and trees, they should be able to meet all their nutritional needs. The key to whole horse health is surely preserving the biodiversity of the fields they graze in, and also their own hindgut microbiome. The Mongolian horses were very skilled at self-selection. The technical name for self-selection is zoo-pharmacognosy. The definition of zoo-pharmacognosy is that the animal (horse) will instinctively choose or seek out which bit of which plant they need to self medicate. The Mongolian horses would nibble a few mouthfuls each of all the different weeds and grasses available, and if we came across a new plant we hadn't seen for a few days, quite often it was the horses who found it first and snaffled a few mouthfuls before the botanist would exclaim in delight and assume the head-down, bottom-up position known to plant geeks the world over.

In human nutrition, we know that almost everything in moderation is good, while anything to excess can be bad, even celery! When you go and see your doctor, they might ask if you are eating your ten portions of different fruit and veg every day, or if you have four varied colours on your plate at dinner. Why would horses be any different? We think we know that bracken is poisonous to horses. But bracken contains an insulin-like compound. Eaten to excess (12kg, the research says) then yes, too much insulin-like compound would be toxic. But in spring, when the lush grass comes through, a little bit of bracken can help the horse cope with the sugar-rich grass flush and protect them against laminitis. Likewise, oak trees and acorns are supposedly poisonous to horses. But oaks contain tannins, which have an anti-helminthic effect. (A helminth is a worm or intestinal parasite.) My horses at home choose to browse the low hanging oak branches in the field, and love to drink out of the tea-coloured stream that runs through the peat bog in the forest. Are they doing their own worm control regime? Or even better, their own probiotic? On advice from the holistic vet, I previously bought some EM1 -Effective Microorganisms, a suspended culture of live bacteria for hindgut health. Drinking from a muddy puddle may well provide the same bacteria, in a handy suspension, at no cost.

Maybe, when horses gorge on acorns, escape from fields or break into feed rooms, it's because they don't have sufficient healthy forage available to meet their needs. Was their paddock bare, had the haynet run out, or were they craving a vital nutrient that cannot be obtained from grass alone? In summer, my horses are kept on a track fenced around the periphery of the field, to limit their intake of lush summer grass. They only break into the middle if the haylage feeders run dry and there isn't enough on the track to interest them. On occasions, when the haylage gets finished overnight but the hedgerow is chock full of fun stuff like blackberries and fresh hawthorn, and the track is covered in tiny bits of green, they don't break through the electric fencing despite the battery being low.

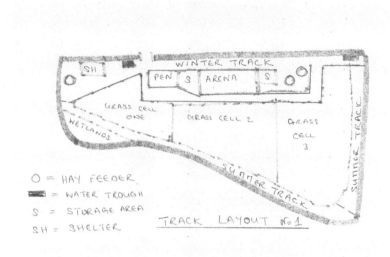

Within the image: SH, WINTER TRACK, PEN, S, ARENA, S, GRASS CELL ONE, GRASS CELL 2, GRASS CELL 3, WETLANDS, SUMMER TRACK, SUMMER TRACK

O = HAY FEEDER
■ = WATER TROUGH
S = STORAGE AREA
SH = SHELTER

TRACK LAYOUT No 1

Track Layout

The question of how much grass your horses need all depends on the quality of your meadow. Maybe a better question would be how many different species of grass-like plants do horses need?

Pause for thought:

- I set you a challenge — how about you go and measure a rough metre square in your horse's grazing or that wild patch in your garden and count how many different species of plant grow there? That would be a lovely place to start.

5

ALBRECHT AND THE AGRONOMIST

O ne of the first jobs on the to-do list when I acquired my own land was to get a full soil analysis done according to Albrecht principles. You may not have heard of Albrecht. I hadn't until I started reading about healthy land. Nor, it would seem, is Albrecht a name familiar to the local Cheshire agronomists.

Albrecht was a pioneering American scientist who surmised and then proved that managing the soil in a way that allowed the soil itself to support a complete ecosystem, not just the monoculture crop currently being grown, would lead to healthier crops, healthier animals and healthier humans. In the long run, healthy, mineral-balanced and aerated soil supports a multitude of plant and other species. A good root system will ensure that the precious soil doesn't get washed away, and a replenished, fertile soil supports various soil-dwelling species, including microbes, flora and fauna. The full soil ecosystem can remain healthy in homeostasis *ad infinitum*. His extensive scientific writings are freely available to buy and make for really interesting reading.

The perpetual delight of becoming a barefoot horse owner is that we have embarked on a daily voyage of discovery towards healthy scepticism and informed self-sufficiency. Once you take the leap of faith and pull the steel horseshoes from your first barefoot horse, with the vet and the farrier and at least half of your friends telling you that it will never work and that you must be mad, once you take that first step from the safety of familiar dogma into novel practice, life will never be the same again. Once you open your mind to the alternative becoming possible, you will have to do a lot of reading, experimenting and research to understand enough about keeping horses healthy enough to flourish barefoot, to deal with the initial difficulties and transition your horse successfully.

With buying my own land came the opportunity to learn how to keep the horses living out all year, as naturally as possible, thriving through a working winter, on a track system, and now, learning about the importance of mineral balance in soil. I absolutely love learning new stuff.

Why do I need to know about soil? Because I am trying to keep healthy horses. Obviously soil quality influences the nutritional content of the grass, and horses eat a lot of grass, so the healthier the grass, the better will be the health of the horses. Their hooves, coats, breathing, gut balance — you name it — nearly every equine (and human) ailment under the sun can be improved by correct diet. And I need to know about healthy soil because the agronomist — let's call him Rick the D@ck — has never heard of Albrecht, or barefoot horses, or indeed of mineral balancing for healthy soil. His area of expertise is how to maximise cash crop yield.

Humans excel in disturbing natural balance. Humans always want maximum yield. We tend to grow a single species grass selected out for the nutrition required to build muscle bulk in animals destined for quick slaughter. In Cheshire we grow ryegrass for fattening and milking cows. Cows are ruminants, horses are not. Horses are neither food nor milk providers, but leisure animals kept to give us pleasure. They evolved to survive in the desert and the steppes, on poor, arid, varied grasslands.

So I got the soil analysis of my field done according to Albrecht principles and the report came back with certain recommendations. I needed Calcined Magnesite (for the magnesium), Potassium Sulphate (for the sulphur) and DAP (Di-Ammonium Phosphate, for the phosphate not the nitrogen). I rang up our local agri-chemical supplier; they very helpfully said I would need to talk to Rick the D@ck the agronomist, who would look at our report and work out which were the best products to fulfil our needs.

Rick had never heard of Albrecht. He looked at the very detailed report and suggested Paddock Royale, a common fertiliser suitable for pony paddocks and readily available at reasonable cost. It would provide all the elements the soil needed, albeit not in the perfect ratios. Great, I thought, I have good land, it doesn't need much; winner winner!

Then Stacey, my neighbour and a kindred soul who had also had an Albrecht soil analysis done, needed specific products and so got him to look at her report. Now I happened to know, having already compared notes, that her soil was completely different to mine, with different issues and very different minerals required to balance her soil. Yet Rick the D@ck recommended exactly the same product for Stacey as he had for us. At which point, alarm bells rang.

Then followed two weeks of intense wrangling. I had to brush up my A-level organic chemistry in order to deal with Rick the misogynist agronomist who finally threw up his hands and said I'll sell you whatever you like. I replied that this was exactly my understanding of how any customer-client relationship would work; I'm still not sure why it took two us weeks to get to that point. Something to do with commission payments I'm sure. Eventually he arranged to have our products mixed, as instructed, and delivered it to the farmer who would do the spreading, albeit covered in warning labels and with an extra special letter spelling out the risk of deadly laminitis in our horses if the mixed product was spread at my requested rate of coverage!

Obviously Rick didn't take in any of the information I shared with him about ratios, didn't understand that the aim was to change the mineral balance of the soil rather than fertilise the grass, nor had he listened to the explanation that the horses will be kept on a track system around the periphery of the field, and therefore not be eating the rich grass at all over the dangerous summer months. He didn't bother to read more or look up Albrecht because obviously he already knows everything he needs to know for the rest of his life.

By contrast, the farming contractor who did the spreading of the chemicals was fascinated by the whole process. He also put down a stone hard standing area for the hay feeders, so the horses could get out of the deep mud in winter. I used to pass his truck parked in my field gateway while he proudly checked his square to see how it was holding up to heavy use, and inspected the horses and the grass.

Pause for thought:

- How healthy is your soil?
- Have you ever checked the mineral balance as well as the nutritional value of your grass or hay?
- Have you ever just spread some lime or fertilised the grass because that is what the farmer recommended, without considering the wider issues?
- Have you considered the soil, rather than the crop, as its own ecosystem that also needs nurturing?

Further Reading;

Albrecht, William A., *Albrecht on Soil Balancing: The Albrecht Papers, Volume 7*, Acres USA (2008)

6

GROW YOUR OWN

W hen you can't get hold of the organic, non-GMO, low-sugar forage you need for healthy barefoot horses, one alternative is to grow your own, if you are lucky enough to own your land. I am very fortunate: I have a consistent supply of organic meadow haylage from a local producer large enough to keep our little herd going all winter, although it does come close some years. It simply hadn't occurred to me that I could make my own haylage from the relatively small area of grass in the middle of the track. After initial experiments, I had settled on a routine of keeping the horses on a fenced track around the edge of the field in summer, while growing the grass in the middle long for winter foggage, also known as standing hay. Our first haylage harvest occurred in the horses' third year of living on the field.

Over the last couple of years, I have learned more about how natural biodiversity in the horse's diet is vital for good hindgut function. I have been following the leading research from Dr Carol Hughes of Phytorigins, who uses the wild Carneddau ponies of North Wales and their environment as a source of inspiration and study. Carol is really generous with her knowledge and shares much priceless information on her Equibiome page. Sarah at Forageplus has also been a big part of my learning journey; it was she who introduced me to the work of Albrecht. Forageplus offer a soil testing service and advice on soil mineral balancing to Albrecht principles. As far as I know, they are the only company in the UK to offer this service. Despite Rick the D@ck's best commission-chasing efforts, we did annual soil tests and treatments as per the Albrecht recommendations for two years. I had given myself a budget break the third year, because treating your land isn't a cheap fix, although it is much cheaper than vet's bills!!

I had also been reading about rewilding and the remarkable ability of the land to heal itself if left alone. Our land would have started life as a lowland hay meadow, with a bit of mere and moss thrown in. A work colleague recently bought a retirement cottage in North Wales with a three acre native upland hay meadow which also happened to be a site of Special Scientific Interest. Talking over coffee about the stringent recommendations he had to follow for the preservation of this now incredibly rare habitat made me think — could I get our field nearer to its original ecological state? And how much healthier for our horses would that be?

The first recommendation is to eschew chemical fertilisers or weedkillers. In fact we were to encourage and embrace plant diversity. All weeds were now welcome, requiring another huge shift in mindset. My mother is a keen amateur gardener and I spent many childhood hours on my knees, weeding for pocket money. My colleague brought me a big bag of grass seeds from his field in Wales (much hilarity in the coffee room ensued), and I also purchased some native wildflower seeds and a native grass mix. Next: a single cut, followed by grazing, but the grass clippings must be cleared, not allowed to rot and thereby fertilise the field. Regular aeration is also required. Spiking the land seems to be the hardest job to convince a farm contractor to do, but it is vital as it gets oxygen into the soil for the roots and the root-dwelling organisms to prosper. After the grass has been cut and cleared, grazing by herbivores is allowed and their dung should be harrowed or spread over the field. The grazing herbivores should not have been treated with chemical wormers as these will kill the dung eating insects.

An aside here: I don't use chemical wormers on my horses unless absolutely necessary. I perform three-monthly faecal egg counts and send off tapeworm saliva tests twice a year. A word of caution though — until a reliable, economic test exists for encysted redworm in equines, the winter worming dose that eradicates the encysted red worm before their possible emergence back into the gut in spring remains essential, in my opinion.

So, what changes have I noticed in my lowland meadow with this regime? I had over ten species of grass that I, the novice botanist, could differentiate in the field. There was almost no ragwort: in July, I had only found fifteen plants to pull in the improved area. The year before I had dug out about three sacks' worth every few months. The track has a few more tiny rosettes of ragwort, but then the track has not been treated as per Albrecht.

Ragwort is a native plant with bright yellow flowers that is toxic to horses and cattle if ingested in large quantities. You will recognise it from its proliferation on motorway verges or the sides of railway lines. It tends to grow in poor, poached soil and the seeds can lie dormant for many years. Ragwort used to be classed as a nuisance plant and there were fines for not controlling it. Now that we know more about the plant's life cycle and its beneficial effects to some thirty species of insect including the cinnabar moth and the carpenter bee, the fines are gone and control is no longer mandatory. However, farmers still tend to loathe seeing it grow freely. The standing plant, when green, tastes bitter and so horses (and other animals) won't eat it. However if it is cut and dried in hay that bitterness goes away and the plant can be readily ingested, so land owners tend to pull it (or the non-organic will spray fields with Glyphosate to kill it) before the field is cut for hay. As the owner of an equestrian smallholding, I try to control its proliferation out of respect for our neighbouring farmers.

We have lots of new herbs and wildflowers, including the wonderful Prunella Vulgaris, also known as selfheal. The previously worrying expanses of nuisance clover (high in protein and potassium; associated with head shaking and other metabolic problems) were not evident in the third year. Instead, we had swathes of new grass. And we even had enough grass to cut!! I was thinking we would have to pay someone to cut it and take it away as there wouldn't be enough to bale but in the funny spring of 2018, the grass just grew and grew. And then shrank again a bit in the crazy heat.

Nonetheless, it was still worth a go. It didn't look like much once it had been mowed and rowed, but the baler kept spitting out bale after bale. Once the tractor-man had gone home, Ernie and I ran around the field, breathless with excitement, counting, ten, twenty, thirty, each square plastic wrapped bale a treasure, looming up on us out of the dusk like a squat green dinosaur. My heart still swells with ridiculous pride when I happen across the photo of my thirty-three bales of home-grown haylage, all stacked and lined up neatly, ready for winter. At the time, this was at least three months' worth of organic meadow haylage, made at a fraction of the price of buying it in. I was both delighted and gobsmacked. There really is no more satisfying feeling than seeing your own land produce a crop. Although, dear reader, please remember that strictly speaking, our crop is horses, not grass.

Pause for thought:

- If you can't buy what you need, could you find a way to grow your own?

Further Reading;

Tree, Isabella, *Wilding: The Return of Nature to a British Farm*, Picadore (2018)

Jepson, Paul, and Blyth, Cain, *Rewilding: The Radical New Science of Ecological Recovery*, Icon Books (2020)

7

THE JOURNEY OF A THOUSAND MILES

After diet, the next pillar for healthy barefoot hooves is exercise.

The journey of a thousand miles begins with a single step.

This should be the motto of all barefoot horses because, in the absence of disease or injury, and assuming the diet is sufficient, good strong hooves are grown in response to work. It is important for me at this stage to emphasise the difference between barefoot transition, i.e. taking the shoes off; barefoot rehabilitation, i.e. taking the shoes off as a strategy to treat or compensate for pathology (injury or disease); and barefoot maintenance, i.e. working a horse that either has never been shod or has been bare-foot for so long that they are an established, functional, barefoot performance horse.

Strictly speaking even a barefoot transition will require some rehabilitation philosophy — remember that steel rim horseshoes are inherently bad for healthy hoof function and cause the foot to deteriorate over time. That shoes caused this process of deterioration used to be common knowledge. Bracy Clark (1771-1860) was an English veterinary surgeon who specialised in conditions of the hoof, and he wrote extensively in books and pamphlets about the harm caused by shoeing. Although he had his own detractors at the time, it is his writings and the recommendations therein that informed the Victorian tradition of taking the shoes off and giving all horses six weeks off work every year. This beneficial tradition has lost traction in modern times.

The needs of the three groups of horses will be broadly similar: a good diet, and as much work as they can tolerate. But how we embark on the journey of a thousand miles might differ slightly in each scenario. In the wild, tracking studies have shown that horses will travel an average of fifteen to twenty kilometres a day just going about their usual daily business, and they will travel up to fifty-five kilometres over twelve hours to get to a watering hole in arid living conditions. The average horse walks out at around six kilometres an hour, so daily that's the equivalent of two and a half hours of brisk walking as a baseline.

Your standard leisure horse at a livery yard in his individual little square paddock with green grass on tap will not be walking anything like that distance. Even on an imaginative and well designed track system around the edge of a grass field, I'm not sure they would need to go half that far.

How far do our horses travel when ridden? An hour's work might include twenty minutes of trot at fifteen kilometres an hour, a maximum ten minutes of controlled cantering and some walking. I would say a generous estimate of an hour's work in the life of the average pleasure horse is probably about seven kilometres, half the distance they would do in the wild on their own, and this level of work generally doesn't occur every day. Use your phone as tracker to see how far you really ride on any given day. I was profoundly disappointed when I started tracking my rides.

The best quality hooves are generally those that work the

hardest. Hooves grow in response to stimulus, so the more stimulus there is, the more hoof wall they will grow. Hooves are stimulated to grow in response to wear. A horse that does many miles of tarmac every week will have established a growth cycle sufficient to keep up with the wear. If the workload is suddenly reduced these horses are commonly reported to need trimming every few days until the hoof adapts to the reduced workload.

Some horse owners report that their horses' hooves actually wear away if they do too much work on tarmac. This is a reason frequently given for why barefoot didn't work for them. They actually say the hooves were wearing away to stubs! There is a reason for this, but it is based on a misapprehension. Look at pictures of wild pony hooves, or donkey or zebra hooves. Then look at the hooves of the shod horses you know. An untrained eye can see the difference, maybe more clearly if you look carefully, without prejudice or preconception.

The shod hooves that we are used to seeing are inherently unhealthy. Compared to the natural functional hoof, shod hooves have long, tall heels, are rimmed with edges of hoof wall that sit proud of the frog and sole, have a hairline that doesn't reach the ground, and often have suboptimal hoof angles that differ between front and back. The first stage of adaptation to barefoot husbandry that the uncertain and anxious owner will notice is that the excess hoof wall breaks away in chunks, the back of the hairline approaches the ground and the digital cushions at the back of the hoof build up substance. As the whole hoof becomes shorter and more compact, as the heels and soles beef up and increase their area of contact to the ground, this could look like the outer hoof wall is wearing away. It is all a matter of perspective. This adaptation process is actually the previously unhealthy hoof correcting itself and preparing to work properly. But if you have taught your mind and eyes to believe that the tall, neat tin-can-horseshoe in a fresh set of shoes is a thing of beauty, that picture in your head will need adaptation too.

The more work the horse does, the better the blood circulation around the foot, the quicker the hoof grows and the better the quality of both horn and sole. This is why so many top endurance horses do so very well barefoot. They do enough miles to grow good hooves, get the benefit of growing self-maintaining hooves and, without steel horse-shoes, there is less wear and tear on the precious legs above due to the natural shock absorption performed by the flexible hoof structures.

It is important that we don't force an uncomfortable horse to move. That is obviously counterproductive, as well as cruel. A sound horse freshly out of shoes should be able to move comfortably on a good artificial surface, soft turf and on super smooth tarmac. If they can't do this then my experience suggests that there must be a previously undetected problem, either in the foot itself or higher up the leg. These are the horses that might need investigating for sub-clinical laminitis (a dangerous inflammatory condition that shows up most in the feet) or other issues.

Some surfaces are surprisingly hostile. Sand with variable hard chunks in it can be a very disconcerting surface. Examples near us would be the red quarried sand walkways at our local training facility and the local surfaced winter farm ride. Cal hates both of these surfaces, as they give way unpredictably under his foot until the sole hits an unyielding stone. I always boot him up for the winter farm ride now. Yet he will eat up the miles on grass, super smooth tarmac, and very fine crushed stone.

Initially, we might have to find creative ways to get the miles in and get those feet started on the journey of a thousand miles. Removing the weight of the rider is a simple and effective way to permit the horse to work in greater comfort. Groundwork is also an invaluable rehabilitation tool. Long lining and working the horse in hand from the ground allows us to observe and to influence the nuances of how the horse uses his body.

When I transitioned Paddy, my first barefoot horse, we were on a polo livery yard. The roads in that area at that time were terrifying glass-like tarmac. There were routes with inclines that I would actively avoid when he was shod. Suddenly, without slippery steel horseshoes, these routes became safe for us to use and the mirror smooth tarmac turned out to be the perfect surface for barefoot hoof conditioning. The main canter track around the local common was fine sand, a great surface to work on comfortably with the added advantage of exfoliation and thrush elimination. Within three months Paddy was not only sound on the easy surfaces but trotted without hesitation at full speed up the limestone hardcore driveway. And he was super fit.

If the horse really can't move freely once the steel shoes are removed, then foot protection should be considered. By hoof protection I mean hoof boots and pads. The paint on Hoof Armour resin looks interesting, as do some of the clip-on plastic shoes, but I do not include steel horseshoes in the category of hoof protection. Anything that impairs the natural physiological function of the hoof cannot be called protective. A sound barefoot horse should step out confidently and comfortably, and the hoof should land heel first on the flat.

Hoof boots have improved exponentially over the last few years. Hoof boots are like trainers (or sneakers) for horses. Usually made of tough rubber, they can be worn just for work so the horse all has the benefits of avoiding nailed on steel horseshoes but can be a little more comfortable on various surfaces when ridden. Paddy made the transition from shod horse to barefoot legend so easily that he never needed any hoof boots. When I transitioned Cal, it was a slower process. The only boots that fitted his enormous Irish feet were Old Macs — they were extremely tough and effective for allowing movement, but they were also heavy and clumsy. They were great for general work but tended to fly off at canter, and I never felt like they fitted well enough to be confident to do any proper jumping. I then tried Cavallo Treks. These were much easier to get on and off but also tended to twist around at speed and still didn't feel secure enough for jumping. Renegade Vipers are the hoof boot version of Jimmy Choos, used by all the winners of the legendary Tevis Cup endurance race in America, but, as an American brand, they just didn't come in daft draught sizes.

Then along came Scoots. These were a revelation. Cal is in the largest size (9), and they don't go on his feet easily towards the end of a trim cycle. But once on they fit well enough to gallop and jump, which means we can hack around the challenging stone tracks in the forest to get to all the good jumping logs and canter areas tucked away in the back corners.

Another way to increase movement is to make sure that the horse does some work without you. A simple twelve-meter-wide track system established around the periphery of the field will increase the miles the horse travels during turnout, compared to a square paddock, particularly if we deliberately station the water trough and the hay feeder at opposite ends of the tracked area. I'm not keen on the routine use of automatic horse walkers because we cannot influence how the horse moves whilst on the walker. All we are achieving is fitness: simple forward motion for a set time. However Emma, my trimmer, tells me about a set of client horses that go on the walker regularly; they have great hooves, suggesting that any movement is good for developing good strong feet even if that movement is not done in the best posture.

To summarise, comfortable movement is key for healthy bare-foot hooves, as well as for healthy brains and bodies. The journey of a thousand miles should take you to a set of super duper bare-foot hooves, assuming that the diet is good enough for that horse and also that there is no underlying pathology or metabolic challenge. Achieve movement in as many different ways as possible: turnout, ridden work, ground work, in hand work, even the use of a horse walker. All these can help you get to an adequate mileage.

If hoof protection is required, then by all means use it to help you get the mileage up. And see if you can find a mindset where you play around and have fun with your horses. The journey of a thousand miles is a long way, and a long time; best if we can all have some japes along the way.

Pause for thought:

- I challenge you to log your rides.
- What is your weekly distance?
- What surface is your horse mostly working on?
- How comfortable is he on these surfaces?
- Do you know how the foot lands?
- Does he land heel first?

YOUR HORSE NEEDS SHOES AND PADS…
OR DOES HE?

The journey of a thousand miles should take you to a set of super duper barefoot hooves, assuming that your horse has no underlying dietary or metabolic challenge, nor any pathology. The lessons that I have learned in my quest to fulfil those two simple conditions form the very basis of this book.

Whereas Paddy sailed through transition really quickly to grow stonking, rock-crunching hooves, Cal has never been an easy barefooter. I decided to get his feet X-rayed a few years ago. He was sore on stony ground, stopping when jumping, a bit stuffy generally. He was beautifully sound on grass, soft ground and smooth tarmac in all three gaits. He had some white line separation, and long toes that seemed to take off forwards within a day or two of being trimmed. He didn't have prominent event lines, so I knew the management of his diet and environment was tight enough, but somehow not good enough for him to grow super hooves.

The vet who did the X-rays said, Your horse needs shoes and pads in order for him to increase sole thickness, and recommended a rest from work while the feet grew. He also suggested taking the toe right back.

Now, as an expert in my own field of colorectal surgery, I do not gratuitously ignore the expert advice of others, but I do want to know exactly what benefits they expect to see from the recommended interventions.

Let's take those sweeping recommendations one at a time.

A rest from work while the feet grow. We know now from our barefoot experience that a hoof needs stimulus to grow. Stimulus requires movement. We also know that horses need movement to thrive: a stabled horse is a compromised horse. So I ask: What sort of rest from what sort of work? Walking around a field grazing is essentially rest for a horse. Anything involving less freedom is confinement and therefore not particularly restful for the horse, either mentally or physically. Please don't get me wrong, confinement might be required if weight-bearing or walking is to be prevented but we must be clear, for a flight animal, what we call stable rest is actually confinement. Prevention of weight bearing or walking clearly wasn't the requirement here. So my version of rest is as much movement as is comfortable and safe. Cal lives out in the field twenty-four hours a day, seven days a week. Without work, that is rest.

Your horse needs shoes and pads. Why shoes? And why pads? And do the two always need to go together? What were the pads for?

The function of therapeutic pads, apparently, is to provide constant, even stimulus to the sole to which the horse's foot will then respond by growing a thicker sole (or just laying down a thick layer of false sole, but that is a whole other dilemma I won't address here.) By improving comfort and thereby increasing ease, we can then hopefully improve the quality as well as quantity of movement. I consulted both farriers and barefoot trimmers and all agreed on the aims and effectiveness of this intervention. So, the killer question: do the pads really need to go under steel rim horse-shoes or is there another effective way of padding the soles? Surely pads can also go in hoof boots? The most time-efficient method was clearly permanent padding to grow sole as quickly as possible. Shoes are obviously one solution. There are all sorts of shoes that can be applied to fix padding to the hoof — from full steel to plastic Cytek glue-ons. I didn't want to put nails in the feet we have spent three years getting as strong as possible out of shoes. And glue-ons apparently aren't a great solution in our wet UK climate. So really, to hold the pads on, we needed hoof boots that could be worn 24/7.

Until I found Scoot Boots, a relatively new brand from Australia, this plan would have been impossible for us. Only a few brands of hoof boots are made in sizes that accommodate the enormous daft draught feet, with no room for thick therapeutic pads The previous clunky boots I had found in Cal's size would have rubbed his heels raw in a few days or spun off in the field and got lost. However, the newly discovered boots were light, made of flexible rubber that didn't rub, didn't hold excess water, didn't seem to trap stones or dirt, and managed to stay put in all but the roughest horse play in deep mud. Cal wore his hoof boots and his therapeutic pads continuously for most of three months. He had a couple of weeks without them when the mud got very deep and then another week off when I was awaiting delivery of replacement pads. He had a few days off work but was so comfortable in his boots that we just went for it-the only way to ensure horses do decent mileage is to do some of it with them. As I may have mentioned previously, the best barefoot performance feet are always those that do twenty to thirty miles a week, ideally on bouncy tarmac to stimulate growth.

I didn't jump him for a few months once I had seen those X-rays, but we walked, trotted and cantered in our hoof boots all over Delamere and Cheshire, and schooled diligently doing our Classical Riding homework. It seemed that Cal was determined to make me complete the journey to training a finished dressage horse, without any pesky eventing distractions. He was also determined to teach me to trim — those toes needed weekly attention to keep them back under control. But that is another story.

I will confess I was nervous when Cal went back for the second set of X-rays. Had I wasted three months being stubborn? Should I just have had him shod? I knew he was no worse, and in many ways he was much better, bouncing around on tarmac, cruising slowly over stones, but I wanted to see a better toe angle and a thicker sole to give me the confidence to persevere with the alternative plan. Thankfully the X-ray evidence was clear: our strategy was working. So my horse didn't need shoes, but he did need pads.

Educate yourselves, question everything, learn about alternatives. The vet wasn't wrong, he just had a huge experience of traditional remedial farriery methods and very little experience of alternative barefoot rehabilitation. I'm sure he had no idea that this positive effect could be achieved without shoes for support. And how could he learn any different if he always recommends shoes?

I was delighted, but not smug. I'm just glad it worked, and that I was happy to spend the time putting the slow miles in and not leaving the ground too often. In my previous incarnation, before Paddy had voted so clearly with his feet, I'm not sure I would have been brave enough to make that choice.

Further Reading;

Nicholas, Lucy, *The Barefoot Horse: An Introduction to Barefoot Hoof Care and Hoof Boots*, JA Allen (2012)

9

MY HORSE WON'T COPE BAREFOOT

My horse won't cope barefoot. I would like a pound for every time I have heard this statement. I'm pretty sure every healthy horse can cope barefoot. Indeed, I personally am running out of reasons why I might ever put a metal shoe on a horse, but I do know that not every owner can cope with having their horse barefoot.

Barefoot can be a hard choice. I have experienced ridicule, uncertainty and prejudice from the vociferous part of the horsey community which doesn't know any better. Funnily enough, I've found that most lay members of the non-horsey public understand really quickly that wild horses don't wear shoes, so, when they stop to think about it, they are not sure why domestic horses should need them.

It would have been very easy with Cal the daft draught for me to believe that my horse couldn't cope with working barefoot. There have definitely been periods along the way where Cal wasn't managing barefoot. It's been incredibly hard for me to keep looking for the metabolic issue, to get to the diagnosis of the under-lying health problem that is stopping him from being a good rock-crunching barefoot performance horse. There have been numerous times when it would have been easier for me to slap some shoes on and just carry on in the old way, but then I could have missed the gastric ulcers and had even less warning about the Chronic Obstructive Pulmonary Disease (airway inflammation with lots of mucous and tissue swelling causing breathing difficulty). I would never have looked for or treated the borderline Cushings, a disorder of pituitary gland function associated with high excretion of cortisol, the stress hormone. Cushings is more common in older horses, or heavy horses, and can be one of the manifestations of equine metabolic syndrome, a spectrum of diseases associated with maladaption to domestication. Luckily I managed to get Cal's Cushings under control with herbal supplements. But his couple of episodes of mild laminitis could have been fatal.

Many of the ways that we choose to look after horses are for our human convenience and not for the horse's health. I know this. I have been there. I had what I thought of as the best-looked-after polo ponies within the M25 when I was grooming for a high goal team all those years ago. I hated some of the more severe Argentine methods, but I learned a huge amount from the polo itinerants and from other horse people in Australia, Scotland, and Germany. I have continued to listen and learn ever since, with a completely open mind. And I have checked the science, the research and the evidence, as I would for my human cancer patients. We should be in a Golden Age of Horsemanship. We have rigorous scientific methods, amazing equipment and technical tools to analyse and interpret data. We are in a position to test every aspect of horse care and the effects on the horse's health and mental well-being. Unfortunately, much of the science is paid for by those with vested interests, and those who believe they know horses the best rarely feel the need to question their own programming or dogma.

It is difficult for someone who hasn't read about barefoot hoof care properly, or thought to question the status quo, to understand that everything they know about traditional horse husbandry is destined to wreck the healthy hoof. Horses are designed to move, travelling many miles a day in the wild. They are built to trickle-feed on a variety of poor shrubs and grasses. If offered a choice, horses would choose an outdoor life in sociable family groups with lasting relationships and plenty of space to avoid conflict. Horses are simply not engineered to stand overnight in shavings soaked in their own urine and faeces, eat too much sugary starchy food and to go out for a few hours a day in an individual turnout paddock which is full of poisonous monoculture ryegrass. Their mental health is also compromised as they are forced into random social groups dictated by human caretakers, or deprived of crucial social contact and bonding rituals such as mutual grooming, and their exercise is generally limited to a little light work for just a few hours a week.

This chapter was prompted by a friend telling me how their half-thoroughbred horse wouldn't cope barefoot because she has typical thoroughbred rubbish feet. (This stereotype about thoroughbred feet is amazingly widespread.) I understand where she's coming from, because I used to feel the same way. Paddy had the worst feet in Cheshire. Despite industrial amounts of a very expensive biotin supplement, he could never hold shoes and his hoof wall was thin and crumbly.

Plenty of other people have felt the same way, watching their horse with his unconditioned hooves limping across the yard when he loses a shoe. I used to believe the same, until my horse taught me different. How would you manage, if I took your shoes off and asked to you to walk across the yard on hardcore or gravel, without toughening your feet up first? You would stutter in exactly the same way. When I was a child there was a world class athlete from South Africa called Zola Budd. She ran, and won, barefoot.

When I took Paddy's shoes off, many people, including the vet and the farrier, told me that I would find that my horse couldn't cope barefoot. However, it was Paddy who forced me to try barefoot, by nearly killing several farriers, including the horse-whispering blacksmith. And once barefoot, his hooves, his body and his brain improved immeasurably. He became sure-footed, confident and healthier. He stopped rushing his fences and I could feel him balancing his body underneath me.

It took time, in Paddy's case about three months, to get him to rock-crunching go-anywhere status. Now at twenty-four he is sound and still going strong. He had four fantastic seasons eventing barefoot, taught my then husband to ride, hunt and team chase, and subsequently gave my step-daughter the confidence to explore the forest.

Paddy is seven-eights thoroughbred. Hoof health has nothing to do with thoroughbred genes. There is actually no significant genetic difference between all the modern horses around the world. Traits, yes; genetic alteration, no. The only exception to this sweeping statement is Hoof Wall Separation Syndrome in Connemara ponies. This recessive genetic syndrome with tragic physical effects would certainly cause early death in the wild and therefore the aberrant gene would have been weeded out as a disadvantage to survival. Unfortunately, in the domestic Connemara population it still propagates, although reputable dealers now perform gene testing, cull affected individuals and issue certificates with the passport to prove that the animal is free from the condition.

The reason that thoroughbreds were thought to have particularly rubbish feet is based on people's genuine experience. However, thoroughbreds, the breed used for racing, are typically kept confined from a young age, fed starchy food and shod regularly from the age of two. Like the rest of the horse, the bones and the soft tissue structure of the hoof doesn't finish developing until the horse is fully mature. If hoof function is compromised from an early age then of course hoof development will be substandard. The old masters knew this. Alois Podhajsky recommended that mares and foals move daily from night pasture to day pasture along a couple of miles of rough track to help the foals' limbs and feet develop. In the wild, foals hit the ground, stand up, suckle and immediately start travelling with the herd, quickly averaging as much as twelve miles a day in their early lives. In my experience, thoroughbreds grow the best feet of all when transitioned to barefoot. This is because many of them have such a strong forward urge that the miles required are easy to do, and also because they have a really sharp insulin response. They are bred for maximum metabolic efficiency and speed. Once they are on a sugar-free low-starch diet, there is virtually no sugar dysregulation to drive an inflammatory response.

In Arab horse racing it is not uncommon to see horses running barefoot, and there is now increasing awareness among the English thoroughbred racing fraternity of the long-term benefits of barefoot husbandry. There are a couple of high profile trainers doing the early season fitness work, and even successfully racing their thoroughbreds barefoot, including Simon Earle here in the UK. And there are many stories from around the world of retired racing thoroughbreds being adopted and successfully rehabilitated to new lives barefoot.

If you do shoe your horse, he may well stride out confidently over all terrain, but actually he is partially unable to feel his feet. Please be aware that when your horse is shod, you miss many of the early warning signs that he is only just coping with our ever more lethal green, lush, rich British pastures. When your barefoot horse is unusually footsore on stones, that is a valuable early warning sign that the grass has changed. In a shod horse, particularly a well fed, little-worked pleasure horse, in show condition, that overnight flush of grass may cause an attack of full blown laminitis before you realise the danger.

So Cal on his good days is great on smooth tarmac, strides out beautifully on fine gravel and small stones but generally does tend to pick his way carefully and a bit more slowly over larger stones and hardcore. His ears never go back, he doesn't make a pain face, if his foot lands on a sharp stone he hops off it like a sensible pony. Mostly he will choose to use the soft ground at the side of the path on very challenging ground. Some might say that this means my horse can't cope barefoot. We do regular fun rides and affiliated eventing. A standard evening hack regularly involves forty-five minutes around the stone paths in Delamere Forest, with a couple of good long trots and a short canter. Once we turn for home, he always marches back to the house.

Is he lame? Or is he clever?

Further Reading:

Barker, Nic, *Performance Hoof, Performance Horse,* JA Allen (2017)

10

THE PERFECT BAREFOOT TRIM

The perfect barefoot trim is a bit like rocking horse pooh. It is an elusive and illusory premise. There is a very good reason why trim is the fourth pillar of successfully keeping the ridden horse barefoot. (The four pillars of barefoot performance are diet, exercise, environment and, only then, trim.)

Time now for another disclaimer. I am not a trained hoof care professional. I am pretty handy with a rasp, by necessity. I do trim my two working horses as required, and then get some muscle (sorry, a farrier or other trimming expert) in to do a checkup every few months. Over the years I have been the responsible human for quite a few barefoot horses, doing all sorts of work, both in Europe and in Australia, some of those years were a long time before the barefoot movement was even a thing. Through Cal, in the full-on quest for the trimming answer to his barefoot dilemma, I have met more hoof-care professionals than I ever thought possible!

When I look back over the years, I think I have always known at some level that working horses didn't necessarily need shoes. And way back in my youth, I don't remember the horses that didn't wear shoes needing a specialised trimmer. Also, way back in my youth, horses were not shod back to back, month in, month out, without a break, literally for years. In my youth, it was accepted wisdom that horses needed a regular break from work, and one of the key features of that break was to allow them some time out of steel horseshoes for their feet to rest and recover.

We knew from observation and experience that keeping horses too long in steel horseshoes caused damage to the structure and function of the hoof. We didn't shoe our three-year-old horses as soon as they started work. (We didn't start three-year-old horses into solid work either, but that is a whole other soap box.) I looked after some really top class polo ponies in Australia that didn't wear shoes at all, and they were playing fast medium to high goal polo on dirt. And I looked after some really expensive show jumpers on the outskirts of Sydney that were only shod for show season so that they could be studded to jump on grass arenas.

Looking back, I don't think I even met a professional farrier in Australia, despite working as a full-time groom for over a year. My German sister and her friends have trekked hundreds of miles around the forests, all riding unshod horses. The Argentine polo grooms, the Australian farmers and the German adventure riders all had rasps in their grooming kit to tidy up any cracks or splits in the hooves. A quick trim was a routine part of grooming.

The reason that we talk about the trim last of all is because if the diet, exercise and environment are right, then radical trimming can become unnecessary. We can split hairs (or hooves) about the definition of a self-trimming (or self-maintaining) horse, but life is pretty sweet when we achieve this, both for the horse and the human. And if the diet or environment aren't good enough, then specialist or remedial trimming may be necessary to compensate or alleviate pathology to some degree. For example, navicular disease can be successfully rehabbed barefoot, and laminitis both treated and avoided. Nic Barker at Rockley Farm has not trimmed any of her horses for about nine years, and she wrote about this experience in her famous Celery blog post, but I'm still not sure whether this completely hands-off approach is feasible for the majority of horse owners. The tracks at Rockley Farm are pretty unique, as is the rough and wild Exmoor grass in between.

Over recent years, while trying to get Cal's feet right, I have met trimmers trained under all umbrellas: the UKNHCP, the IAEP, trimmers who trained with Jaime Jackson (Mr Paddock Paradise) himself, others who followed KC La Pierre, and a couple of farriers, including one who practises under grandfather rights. I spent years looking for the magic solution, the one person or method that would turn Cal's weird feet over time into nice round hooves that could function better. I drove myself, and many trimmers and hoof care professionals, to distraction. When I met my perfect trimmer, what I found was someone that I could have an ongoing conversation with. We tried every approach; super radical trims every two to three weeks, trying to model the hoof into a specific shape, letting the hoof wall get long to act like a natural version of rim shoes. We tried keeping the toes super short, controlling the flare, leaving the heels, balancing the heels, rasping the heels, taking down the bars, leaving the bars.....

Can I tell you a secret? No matter what we did, the hoof always looked exactly the same two weeks later.

Just as the horse grows enough foot to keep up with the wear created by work, the more you trim a hoof, the more exuberantly it will grow. The more you trim a particular flare, the more the hoof responds, by growing more flare. This is because, for some reason, at that point in time, that flare is needed to provide support. You simply cannot force a challenged hoof into a healthy shape until you remove the stimulus that is preventing the horse and the hoof from being healthy. It seems so obvious now when I write it down in black and white, but it took me many years to accept that truth, and a few more years to convince some of the other key professionals in our horse-care circle.

The fundamental truth is that hooves reflect what is going on in the physiology of the horse. If the horse is footsore, sensitive and tentative on challenging surfaces, there is an issue with the metabolism that has not been adequately addressed. There is inflammation going on somewhere in the body. The sore foot may well be a warning sign of sub-clinical laminitis. Laminitis is a systemic or whole body condition. The horse's feet are the affected end organ, like a diabetic foot in humans. As such, laminitis is not cured by focusing on the foot. The whole body inflammation may require a holistic approach to damp it down. Putting shoes on a sore horse is like putting a sticking plaster on a pressure sore: it hides the wound but doesn't address the problem.

Cal did grow better feet, eventually. Once I had his pro-inflammatory tendency damped down with a diet that was free of starch and sugar, organic, and varied with plentiful antioxidants. Once I knew that we had to avoid combination wormers, fertilised forage and processed food. Once I understood the importance of hindgut health, and the role of the biome in driving or controlling inflammation. After all that, his feet improved immensely.

Inflammation can be addressed from the hindgut first; the more I learn about the biome, the more convinced I am that the answers to many diseases, both horse and human, are to be found in the microbiome. The biome is the name given to the myriad population of bacteria in the hindgut, of horse or human or other animal. There is more genetic diversity in the biome than there is between individuals' DNA signature. And many diseases affect the healthy balance of bacteria in the gut, or are exacerbated by imbalances in the bacterial population. Biome derangement has been linked to inflammatory bowel disease such as Crohn's in humans, to gastric ulcer disease in horses, and even to dangerous behaviour in dogs. Certain species of bacteria proliferate at the expense of others, and the animal's innate ability to self regulate and heal itself is impaired.

If we can sort out the diet and reverse the inflammation then, when the horse is healthy, the feet will reflect the movement patterns of the horse. We can improve movement with correct classical training and bodywork, and the foot will maintain itself in a functional shape that reflects health inside and above. In the meantime, you can trim those flares as much as you need to but, until the loading pattern from above is altered, the wear pattern will persist and the flares will keep coming back. This stage is a bit chicken and egg: you may need to keep the flares under control to allow correct loading of the limb while the horse develops and changes.

So trim as much as you need to, and as little as you can get away with. Take frequent photos and video. And if the feet aren't performing, don't just keep blaming the trim, sort out the rest of the horse first. SERIOUSLY. That particular nugget has taken me six years to understand, accept, and completely internalise as a guide to keeping my horse well. True rock-crunchers are a joy to behold, but not all horses will get there whilst living in England's pleasant pastures green, particularly now that pasture is mainly ryegrass, and the use of fertilisers and pesticides has become ubiquitous.

The optimum holistic husbandry regime allows your barefoot horse to be sound, functional, comfortable, balanced and landing heel first confidently on most terrain. Of course there is no perfect barefoot trim. But once the diet, exercise and environment are in balance, then the hoof will be healthy and we should be able to trim as little as possible and as rarely as required.

Further Reading:

Jackson, James, *The Natural Trim*, J. Jackson Publishing (2012)

11

ANOTHER SELF-TRIMMING HORSE

Finally, after owning Cal for seven years, after all the trials and tribulations, I was very proud and pleased to announce that I had another self-trimming horse! And once it became a reality, I'm wondering why it took me so long to understand that even funny feet Cal could be a self-trimming horse.

For any self-respecting hoof nerd, a self-trimming horse is the ultimate aim. The self-trimming horse has a perfect balance between wear and growth, balances his own feet through work to the shape that suits him, and is sound in the work he does. I never thought Cal could be a self-trimming horse until my barefoot life seemed to come full circle.

I've written about how my barefoot journey began, and about my trials and tribulations with funny feet Cal, including the point where I thought we had really cracked it but, all along, I was operating from within a false paradigm, despite hoof-geeking obsessively all these years. I thought a horse's hooves had to be good before he could become a self-trimming horse.

In the early days, in ultra-traditional pony club horse counties like Cheshire, barefoot horse owners were considered eccentric freaks. Sarah, the pioneer barefoot trimmer in our area, drove around the county to trim her clients' horses with a huge tub of magnesium oxide in the back of her jeep and a set of scales. Who knows what the police would have made of her white powder delivery round? We didn't know as much about best nutrition for healthy feet as we do now, although we knew diet was the key. As was exercise. When I transitioned Paddy he was being looked after by Mel the polo groom. He did at least five miles daily, plus whatever I did with him in the evenings and weekends. And luckily, due to the facilities locally, he was able to do that comfortably from the first day his shoes came off. Glass smooth tarmac really is the best surface for conditioning rock crunching feet! Hoof boots were really hard to buy, really clumpy and mostly imported from America and made for little horses with dainty feet. I didn't buy any for Paddy. He never needed them.

Then along came Cal. He arrived from Ireland in the most horrific set of shoes. Looking back I'm really not sure how I didn't spot the very funny feet. The whole of the hoof capsule sat in front of the cannon bone! During his first six months with me, he fractured a carpal bone (in shoes) tripping over that toe. The moment his box rest was over, he started his barefoot rehab.

Environment is also key. Once I had my own six-acre field which I could proudly put a track around, I started creating my very own paddock paradise. I finally had complete control of my horses' diet and lifestyle. I could mineral balance to a steady supply of late cut meadow hay, and then later haylage. I tested the soil and then applied the recommended chemicals according to the Albrecht protocol. The location of our new home meant we did our rock-crunching mileage around fabulous Delamere Forest and the surrounding area.

And I kept searching for the elusive perfect trim that would finally turn Cal's peculiar set of feet into something functional. I sought advice from an entire posse of trimmers over the first few years. One got very busy with her supplement business. The next wasn't flexible enough to fit in around my hectic work schedule. The third was great but then got poorly and needed a couple of operations. I went back to a UKNHCP trimmer for an alternative view. That alternative then moved down south. I sought a couple of further opinions, one of whom did a really radical trim which left him sore for weeks. Then I eventually met Emma, who is a good listener, really knows her nutrition and is always keen to discuss with and learn from all horses and clients. She is also good friends with Nick Hill and Ralitsa, the holistic vet, so we got the benefit of three heads to scratch.

Emma and I worked together and kept talking and experimenting. We went through gentle trims, more invasive trims, leaving the flares, taking the flare off, trim the bars, leave the bars, attack the toe, swipe the heels, and on and on. Yet, no matter what we tried, the feet improved a bit month by month but remained stubbornly slipper like, with thin soles, shallow collateral grooves and little heel height.

Cal was surprisingly functional over the years, despite the feet looking flat and poor. He has worked hard on all surfaces except stones and we have had some great fun. Then Emma went on a workshop with Nic Barker of Rockley Farm and Feet First fame, and my barefoot life came full circle. Any self-respecting hoof nerd will know of Nic's seminal blog piece, Celery: briefly the upshot is that, if everything else is good, trimming is unnecessary and we should allow the horse to grow the hoof he needs.

I always have believed in self-trimming horses, and in fact have met many over the years. Paddy was essentially self-trimming apart from a check every three months and a quick touch-up for trips out, and Rocky looks like he will go the same way but, for some reason, it had never occurred to me with Cal. How could those ugly, pathological-looking feet possibly become healthier without shaping help?

Luckily, Emma is a good listener. She came back from the workshop and basically waved a rasp at all three horses. And told me to get out there and work them and see what occurs. And guess what? Cal finally grew the feet he needed. They weren't pretty. There was lots of bar. He obviously needed it. The white line opens up again more or less straight away after a touch-up in summer. When you look at the top it looks like there is excessive flare but, when you pick the foot up, on the view from the bottom they are actually not too bad.

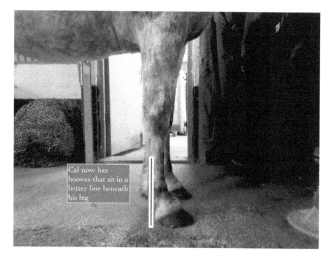

Cal now has hooves that sit in a better line beneath his leg

Better Hoof

The toe always looks like it needs to come back, and it does, so I give it a few gentle swipes with a rasp every time I ride. But the new and exciting development from the less-is-more approach was the increase in the depth of the collateral grooves. I'm not saying he'll never get trimmed again. Those toes need touching up, as do any cracks and chips. But what we found was that the more we trimmed, the more hoof he grew, and it was always exactly the same foot that grew back. Now that we are not trimming so persistently, the foot is growing more slowly but is also building itself up, from the inside. And so I've come full circle, back to Celery — in a healthy horse, barefoot is never all about the trim. I think I finally have a healthy horse. That's been another journey, getting the diet right-and now that we have stopped messing around trying to fix his feet, we seem to have acquired another self-trimming horse.

Until you've seen a horse move and the way the hoof lands, you cannot judge the level of function. Bear this in mind and ask yourself — is your horse self-trimming? Does he land heel first? If not, have you ever thought that less could be more?

Further resources:

Barefoot slow motion film from Rockley Farm:
https://youtu.be/SJKom2Pdbds
HD Slow motion footage —
the horses have had damage to navicular, DDFT,
collateral and impar ligament and other injuries and
are now working barefoot

12

BIG, FIT HORSES CAN GET LAMINITIS TOO

Laminitis is a common, painful and often recurrent condition in domesticated horses, ponies and donkeys. It is caused by a sugar or starch overload often associated with turnout on lush pasture in spring or autumn. It is a severe inflammatory condition, of which the effects are most noticeable in the tissues (laminae) bonding the hoof wall to the pedal bone inside the hoof. In serious cases, the disease can result in the pedal bone sinking or rotating within the hoof under the weight of the horse, sometimes to the extent that the sole of the foot is penetrated by the pedal bone.

Laminitis can be a death sentence. More than seven percent of equine deaths are linked to laminitis, with severely affected animals having to be euthanised. Laminitis is not just a disease affecting small, chubby, native ponies: big, fit horses in medium work can get laminitis too, as I discovered to my chagrin a couple of years ago.

I was chatting about our recent troubles at the area qualifiers and the lady I was talking to said, Oh, he's a big horse, we forget they can get laminitis too. In the accepted dogma, laminitis is mainly a disease of the small native ponies, bred to survive on the moors and fells, good doers, horses that make the most of every mouthful of food and seem to get fat on fresh air.

Cal is a good doer, but he is also a big, fit horse in medium level work and had been out eventing the week before he reminded me that big fit horses in proper work do indeed get laminitis too.

The most common cause of laminitis is now known to be metabolic, either associated with Equine Metabolic Syndrome (a sort of type II Diabetes for horses) or Equine PID, more commonly known as Cushing's disease. Metabolic causes means that laminitis is a systemic disease, in other words, a disease of the whole horse. As such, neither the cause nor the treatment are limited to the foot.

I'm pretty sure Cal has Equine Metabolic Syndrome, although I've never tested him properly. How do I know this? Because at various times over the years, he has been a tricky horse that has often struggled to work hard barefoot on all terrains. For those of you who do not fully embrace the barefoot concept, let me share with you my paradigm. Any horse with the correct diet, environment, exercise and trim should be able to go without steel horseshoes and work hard barefoot. Those four simple-sounding words are not always simple things to achieve in our green and pleasant land. Cal is an Irish Sports horse, ergo he is half Irish Draught, and he looks like he got quite a bit of Connemara in the mix, so a dose of Spanish blood too. (The exact origins of the Connemara pony are uncertain, but the Connemara pony was mainly influenced by Scandinavian and Spanish blood. Legend has it that the breed originated in 1588 when the Spanish Armanda ran aground on the west coast of Ireland. Their Andalusian horses were let off loose and they began to breed with the wild horses of Ireland.)

He didn't get much of the thoroughbred racehorse in his phenotype, that's for sure. Cal's metabolism is finely tuned to survive in the Irish peat bogs, or possibly also in arid Spanish scrubland. I make sure he doesn't get much of our green grass of

Cheshire: a mere sniff makes him footsore so a good belly-full would probably be the end of him. He is the main reason why all my horses are mostly track dwellers, and his story is a vital part of how I came to buy the big house and my own land, because traditional livery yards simply could not cater for his needs. This horse loves fresh thistles, bashes down nettles to let them wilt, eats a bit of bracken for the insulin-like compound, and goes mad for ivy, again for the sugar busting properties. He is pretty good at managing his own condition, as long as he is offered the variety of herbs and plants he needs to offset the green poison. He gets a small bucket feed which contains salt, a hindgut balancer which is formulated to feed a good balance of different bacteria, and another plant-based supplement with lots of antioxidants designed to support the immune system and homeostasis of tricky metabolic horses.

He lives on a track system. His main needs — friends, forage and freedom — are met as best we can. He lives out in my field all year round, in a stable social bubble with his mates, to groom, play, commune with and boss around. The horses have access to constant ad lib forage, and are, I hope safe from stress. As he is pretty dominant, Cal is the safest of all from stress, especially as Paddy is the lookout.

As for exercise, he's my main horse. As I said, he lives out in the fenced-off track around the edge of the field, so he does about five miles a day mooching around on there. He also gets ridden three to four times a week: a mixture of hacking, schooling, jumping, with some fast work every ten days or so. Of course he could do more, if I had more time. I have found another rider to help me with him this year, and his feet are lots better for the extra miles.

With him, the trim has always been tricky. But that's mainly because Cal has been so tricky metabolically. The more I learn about feet, the more I think the difference between a good trim and a bad trim is a bit like a haircut: two weeks! As I said in the previous chapter, bad feet are impossible to trim into a healthy shape and function, and good, healthy, working feet are really hard to trim into a bad shape because they just wear themselves correctly with work and movement.

Cal has been footy on stones for his entire barefoot career. We use nice little euphemisms but make no mistake, a slightly sore foot is a slightly weak or a pathological foot. That's why I would never call a horse sound unless it was truly sound without shoes: if the horse is sore when you take the shoes off, the shoes are disguising a problem. It took me a good few years of looking at hoof photos to realise that Cal was actually a sub-clinical laminitic.

When I first bought him his feet ran so far forward, like Turkish slippers, that the whole foot sat in front of a plumb line dropped down his cannon bones, yet he was "sound as a pound" in shoes. When he broke his carpal bone and we took the shoes off it took three full years of barefoot rehabilitation to get to a stage where he actually had some foot under the same plumb line dropped from the cannon bones, and four years to get the heel bulbs back so they are in line with the middle of his cannon bones, like a correct confirmation picture in a text book.

The under-run heels, the slipper-like toes, the occasional growth ring, these were all stigmata of the borderline laminitic. Yet he had worked hard, team chased, hunted, evented, with the only sign of challenge occurring on very stony ground. So many people said I should just shoe him, as he limped over the stones, as if that would solve all our problems, and that advice even came from some barefoot trimmers and vets. Had he been shod, I might not have spotted this relatively mild attack of laminitis until it was a full-blown disaster.

I had brought him down to the house to get him ready to compete that weekend. We were due to travel down south for the national Express Eventing championship. I had ridden him in the arena, sharpening him up ready for the competition, then bathed him, cleaned all the tack and left him in the stable for an early start. Normally, when down at the house, the horses get a couple of flakes of low-sugar, high-fibre haylage, but our local shop had run out so I had bought a small bale of a different brand of haylage instead. I gave the now spotless Cal a good feed and a good big section of haylage to last him overnight. The next day he was sore, pointing a foot at me, and shifting his weight around behind. There would be no championship fun for us that weekend.

It took me a few days to twig what was going on: because one foot seemed to be worse, I thought it was an abscess first of all. And I was still feeding the new brand of innocuous-looking haylage. It was only when I read the small print on the label and realised it was ryegrass haylage that I put two and two together. After a few days staying down at the house, no abscess had appeared and Cal wasn't actually a welfare case so I moved him back to the field. He got better there, but after ten days was still not looking rideable. He had palpable pulses in all four legs, was moving very slowly, and appeared miserable.

I got the vet out, who agreed with me that it was laminitis, but very mild. It was so hard to spot that the vet said, a lot of owners wouldn't have noticed there was anything wrong. He gave Cal a shot of intravenous analgesia which allowed me to get hoof boots on his front feet so he was comfortable enough to walk back to the house, and then to march him up the big hill. I kept him at the house, rationing every mouthful he ate: no grass at all, a small section of high-fibre haylage or a tiny feed every four hours. I walked him up and down the steep hill twice daily. The purpose of this strict diet and exercise was to sharpen his insulin response again. The enforced exercise had the same effect on me! He had Phytorigins Rescue Remedy, which is a five-day course, a double dose of the hindgut supplement, double dose antioxidants and a sachet of Danilone (an anti-inflammatory pain killer) twice daily.

It was a bad spring. I have another medical friend whose horse got laminitis because she was a bit busy with work and didn't ride for a week: nothing else changed. And I have heard local tales of other big, fit horses in reasonable work who have succumbed to the condition after a seemingly innocent change in diet or management. The grass that spring had been bonkers: wet and warm and then sunny is a great combination for really rich Cheshire cow pasture. Our track looks totally bare sometimes but it's not often the scorching sun that has killed the green stuff; mostly, it is the horses munching away that keeps the grass looking poor.

After four days, Cal was much improved, and he got back to hacking out and schooling again after ten days. He went back to the now very dry, sandy, grass-free track (thanks to that fabulous hot summer of 2018) on about day five (more to do with my work pressure than his precise symptoms). The vet offered to do a glucose stimulation test to see if it was definitely Equine Metabolic Syndrome. I politely declined this. The blood test says it's not Cushings, there is no really effective treatment for EMS other than the kind of tight management which we do already, and there is a significant risk of causing laminitis from the stimulation test.

Since having Cal, my rudimentary knowledge of horse physiology and nutrition is now nearer degree level. Of course it helps that I am already an expert in human physiology, so the proper equine textbooks are understandable to me. I have tried every supplement on the market, tried every supposedly healthy bagged feed, and have come around to the acceptance that maintaining a healthy population of bacteria in the hindgut is the key. Then all that is really required is work, hay, water, salt and enough variety in the horses' environment to allow them to forage for what they need. In the absence of variety, supplements might be required and it's the Phytorigins approach that makes the most sense to the cynical scientist in me.

Prevention is better than cure.

Cal wasn't on anything rich or high in protein or sugar, but I have now cut down significantly from what I was feeding and will cut down even more if he has a quiet week. He wasn't fat at the time, but his condition hasn't really changed on less food so I think feeding the minimum required to keep him fit is definitely the way to go. I now know that every mouthful counts, that I will never switch haylage or anything else suddenly again for my convenience. I know now that this horse needs to work hard every week, no matter how occupied I am with my job. Even in a busy month, he still is an amateur's eventing horse, he will never be in proper hard work like a polo pony or a racehorse.

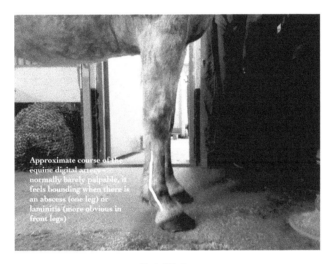

Approximate course of the equine digital artery, normally barely palpable, it feels bounding when there is an abscess (one leg) or laminitis (more obvious in front legs)

Pedal Pulse

Pause for thought:

- Do you check your horse's pedal pulses every day? Whether your horse is shod or not, a palpable pulse might be the first sign of impending laminitis, and feeling a change early might just save your horse from a full-blown attack.
- Do you watch every mouthful your horse eats? Keeping a tricky barefoot horse sound, healthy and in full work is a sure way to turn into a feed geek.
- Do you reduce the bucket feed that day if your horse is doing less work?

Further Resources:

https://www.ecirhorse.org

Jackson, Jamie, *Laminitis: An Equine Plague of Unconscionable Proportions: Healing and Protecting Your Horse Using Natural Principles & Practices*, J. Jackson Publishing (2016)

13

OF COURSE THE ENVIRONMENT MATTERS

I've talked about environment before, but I can't write of it enough. Of course the environment matters for keeping the ridden horse barefoot successfully. By environment, I mean all the places that your horse works, plays and relaxes in.

Ask yourself — where does he spend most of his hours? And how helpful is that particular environment for building high performance barefoot hooves? How many hours does the horse spend in a stable? That's x number of hours he's not moving. It's also x number of hours that he's standing in or on bedding mixed with urine and faeces. And what is the horse eating while standing there? If your horses are the fortunate ones that get plenty of turnout, how many hours is that? What sort of surface are they turned out on? What are they eating while turned out? Are they on a track system or in a small individual paddock square? How many miles do they move while turned out? How far do they have to move for their food and water? And all that is before we consider whether their social and behavioural needs are met.

We know that the horses with the healthiest barefoot hooves are found in feral horse populations. In our part of the UK, our nearest feral population are the Carneddau ponies of North Wales. This ancient herd of ponies are truly wild and have frequented this mountain range in Snowdonia for thousands of years. Their numbers are controlled, but other than that they are not managed in any way. A recent segment in a wildlife programme featured a stallion in his prime chasing off a potential usurper. There were wonderful shots of both ponies cantering effortlessly over the rough, stony ground. The Mongolian ponies had similar skills.

Could you canter over rough ground in your bare feet without any training or conditioning? I know I couldn't, or certainly not straight away. I do spend a lot of my time barefoot, and when I was travelling through Israel and Australia and shoes were mostly optional. I could run miles barefoot on packed dirt and tarmac. But it did take some time to toughen my feet up. This is true for both human and horse. And these days my feet are soft and ouchy again.

If your horse spends most of the time standing in a field of soft mud or working in a soft arena, of course they won't be able to march briskly down a stony track. Just like muscles, bones and tendons, feet also need conditioning. A good diet sets the barefoot horse up for success, while the miles will build and shape the feet, but at the end of the day the feet will perform best on the surface to which they have become most accustomed. If you want your horses to be rock-crunching champions, then they will have to crunch some rocks!! They can be exposed to gravelly then rocky surfaces, bit by bit, building tough feet incrementally. So, of course the environment matters. Track systems in summer are great because they encourage movement, limit grass intake and tend to pack down into hard dirt. You can enrich sections with pea gravel or hard core, best done on the horses' route to a favourite spot so they traverse the surface regularly.

Be realistic when you are out hacking. Build up the exposure to challenging surfaces gradually, initially at slow speeds, and possibly hop off for a challenging section. Let the horse pick their way, slowly if required. One of the major benefits of keeping your ridden horses barefoot is the increase in proprioception and the way that allows them to choose their balance over challenging terrain and protect the joints, if you give them the time to learn the skills. If you only ever work on a beautiful level surface, be that grass, dirt or arena footing, how will your horse learn to dodge tree roots, deal with a steep camber or adapt to undulating terrain? It's like the difference between road running and cross country running — in human terms it's a completely different sport.

Environment matters for both physical and mental health. The way we keep our domesticated horses is profoundly unnatural, even when we are doing our best by them. Low-level stress and gut dysfunction are often contributors to poor hoof performance. As well as the physical, you could think of the hooves as the most sensitive barometer of your horse's mental and psychological health. Does the environment you keep your horse in meet all of their needs? And I don't mean shelter, food and water here. That's the minimum to keep the RSPCA away. I mean the species-specific needs for mental and psychological health.

Pause for thought:

- Is your horse living a full and satisfying life in horse terms?
- Or is he/she being kept alive and functional purely for human use? That is a whole new dilemma!

14

TURNOUT VERSUS LIVING OUT

Here is another phrase that should have made me a million pennies: "My horse could never live out, she loves her stable. She's always begging to come in at night."

Apart from the fact that this begging is actually a learned behaviour, because horses live for routine, we also need to understand that there is a substantial difference between providing a bit of turnout time in a simple square paddock versus allowing our horses to live out full time in a suitable environment that provides for their basic species needs (and rights) of friends, forage and freedom.

Of course I would much prefer that any horse got to spend a measly hour turned out in a small paddock rather than no time out in the fresh air at all. But we must acknowledge that horses are made for and require movement, and that the more they can move, the happier and healthier they will be. And that all our horse-care practices are a human compromise balanced between cost, practicality and ease of use of the animal. Turnout versus living out is a good example of a compromise chosen to benefit the human over the horse. If your horses, in their current living situation, do not have access to regular turnout, then please do find somewhere else to keep them. As chattels or domesticated animals, horse do not have their species-specific needs protected by law. Other equids, in zoo environments, have legal protection that stipulates how much space they need to move around in, and that mandates companionship and the ability to socialise with other individuals of the same species, and insists that they have access to suitable forage and are trickle fed as they require for digestive and mental health. Why should a Przewalskii's horse in a zoo have better living conditions than your precious and much-loved horse of a lifetime?

I tolerate thick mud on my horses from November through to March, and many other days in between. Other than competition days, I only groom when I actually intend to ride. I only wash a tail or tidy up a mane on the days when we have to look presentable to compete. And I am comfortable with those choices. You won't shame me into bathing my horse in winter — he needs the grease in his coat for waterproofing. Likewise, Cal the daft draught gets to keep his full feathers all winter. And I very rarely brush legs — layers of super-dry mud acting as insulating wellies are the best protection against mud fever.

Many people mistakenly believe that how a horse behaves in a limited turnout situation will determine how prepared that horse is to live out full time. But there is a huge difference between limited turnout and living out full time. To understand why, we need to know more about the behaviour of the wild horse.

Horses can tolerate and in fact thrive in a temperature range from zero to thirty degrees celsius. Horses much prefer to be too cold than too hot. They can always warm themselves up, by increasing their activity or by eating plenty of forage that then gets fermented in the hindgut, where the fibre consuming bacteria actually produce heat. Effectively horses, as hindgut fermenters, have their very own central heating system. As long as horses have adequate access to forage, they will keep fermenting that forage and keep themselves warm.

Horses left in their natural state will grow a fabulous winter coat. This has at least two layers: an underneath fluffy insulating layer and a longer, coarser protective layer on top. If you have ever turned your horse out naked in the rain you may have noticed the herringbone pattern that the dried in rain has left. This is no accident. The herringbone acts like a guttering system, allowing the water to run off the top of the coat while keeping the fluff underneath dry. As long as the fluff has enough air in between the hairs, it acts as an amazing insulation layer. It surprises me each time, coming home after work to ride and pulling a full winter-coated but unrugged horse in from the field, to find how dry the horses' backs actually are most of the time.

And all horses can grow a good coat if left to adapt. My old retired Paddy is seven-eighths thoroughbred, thin-skinned with what, to the human eye, looks like a very fine coat. We first moved to our new home from a livery yard in March so the horses were coming out of winter having been clipped and rugged. The second year, I just didn't get around to putting any rugs on. I had the rugs ready in the shed in the field but my little herd never seemed to need them. Paddy grew a good enough coat during his second year in the forest, although he still looked a bit poorer than I would have liked coming into spring. In the third year, a really cold, wet year, he grew the most amazing triple-layered pelt and wintered really well. And has continued to do so ever since.

I trace clip Cal to allow me to work him, but with a shallow trace clip he still doesn't need a rug. He's half Irish Draught so he grows the most beautiful fluffy winter coat and thrives on fresh air. Incidentally, I almost never dry him off after riding. In Delamere I would walk him back to the field from the house so he cooled off a bit; then the first thing he would do when turned out was roll in the cool, sandy mud, which was good for his coat and his body temperature.

When it did snow, the horses loved rolling in the white stuff. It was like a spa day for them. Snow is also strangely insulating — the horses all wore snow rugs when they could, and their backs were toasty warm underneath!

Our field had a wooden shelter, which the horses rarely used, but also really good hawthorn hedges all around the field perimeter, good tree cover in the bottom corner and, most importantly, the field had dips and hollows that offered varying natural windbreaks. The favourite spot was down in the dip in the bottom corner of the field. Eddisbury Hill, with its Iron Age fort, offers a natural wind break and the hollow has quite deep sides and is south-facing. I used to think the horses had all escaped as you literally couldn't see them until you were on top of them, sunbathing down out of the wind.

Each part of the field served a different purpose in their daily routine. The sandy area near the field shelter was the sand rolling area. The steeper side of the slope below the field shelter was the mud rolling area. The horses were very particular in their personal grooming routine. They would do a very thorough sand roll every morning after breakfast. The mud roll occurred in the afternoon generally, as they coated themselves up with extra insulation for the night.

By the way, rolling is also a bonding activity. I discovered this one summer day when I took a book down to the field to sunbathe. I was flat on my back reading and enjoying the damp grass on my sweaty back when all three horses came over to join me for a rolling session. That was a pretty cool moment.

The Pzrewalski horses in Mongolia coated themselves in mud in the morning to keep the midges away but my field didn't have good mud in summer. I could always tell when a cold winter night was due though, because my horses would be coated in mud from eyelash to fetlock. This is even more the case now we are on livery at a different yard, which has much better mud! They never got rain scald: the twice-daily self-grooming regime works much better than the human version. When it rained, they might occasionally hide in the field shelter for a half an hour break if it was really relentless. More often, they would be found grazing down in the dip, or browsing huddled under the hedge. Once there was a lull in the weather, they would charge around a bit to warm themselves up, then get back to the serious business of grazing. They would graze for a couple of hours, then nap, then have some haylage, roll or groom, then go for a wander around the perimeter and stop for a drink. I used to love to spend the hours watching them just being horses.

So, if you believe that your horse is begging to come in at night, ask yourself two questions. Why have you trained that behaviour? And what is missing from that turnout environment that would make your horse less keen to come in?

Does he have friends, forage and freedom? Is there enough stimulation? A place to hide from the sun? A place to shelter? A place to roll? Room to get up some speed and play? A place to look out over the surrounding area?

Now we are back at livery, my three do wait by the gate at the appointed time, expecting to come in. Before we moved back to livery, they used to wait by the gate of the field at 6pm for evening feeds. But they weren't asking to come in. They would eat their dinner, say thank you, and then wander off down the field to the water trough and the haylage feeders. Now they know their new routine — they are coming into a stable for a feed and then spend the night in during the winter or the day in during the summer. The turnout, although lovely, isn't in an environment good enough to support living out all the time. My horses have adapted to a degree of confinement, for now. But when we find our next dream

Nelipot, I'm determined that I'm going to need a school dinner bell to call them down off my big wooded hill.

Pause for Thought:

- What is missing from your turnout environment?
- Does your horse have friends, forage and freedom?
- Is there enough mental stimulation?
- Is there a place to hide from the sun?
- A place to get away from the flies?
- A place to shelter from the rain? A place to get out of the wind?
- Is there a good place to roll? Enough room to get up some speed and play?
- And do they have a high spot, a place to look out over the surrounding area?

Recommended Reading:

Jackson, Jamie, *Paddock Paradise: A Guide to Natural Horse Boarding*, J. Jackson Publishing (2016)

Myers, Jane, *Healthy Land, Healthy Horses, Healthy Pasture: The Equicentral System Series Book 2*, Equiculture Publishing (2015)

15

THE MYTH OF THE ALPHA

I'm learning energy work at the moment. The first few sessions with a new teacher, even one infused to the hilt with energetic information, are always about seeking a common language. No matter how connected or enlightened we are, as humans we still need a framework of communication, and that communication can occasionally be clumsy. Sometimes one might drop a complete clanger. It may occur as an attempt at shorthand, to convey a feeling, or it may reflect confusion stemming from a different understanding of words. My teacher's clanger today was: The horse trusts you. You are the alpha in the herd.

There we have it: the myth of the alpha.

Now first, let me clarify. I'm not bitching here. I spoke up at the time and, between us, we found a different set of words that conveyed the feeling required in the moment. But it did get me to thinking.

The myth of the alpha or herd leader is a strangely pervasive dogma. Depending on who you read, it may be the alpha male, the stallion or herd defender, who fights off all comers to protect his harem of mares and pass on his genes. Or it may be the alpha mare, the real herd leader, who makes all the important decisions in the herd, including when to move and when to drink, eat and sleep. So much training methodology, in both equine and canine training, is based on this flawed concept. We are told we have to become the pack leader, to dominate, to demand respect, if we expect to earn obedience or cooperation. There was a powerful vogue in the natural horsemanship movement which was premised on selling this belief in various shiny, guru-based guises. Control the feet and you control the horse; the use of pressure-release; the round pen work; and join up, the latter made famous by Monty Roberts. The more enlightened practitioners have thankfully now moved beyond dominance training. Nor was the use of dominance limited to the natural horsemanship cowboy training methodologies. Much of the more traditional British equestrian teaching also assumes the use of casual, matter of fact coercion in training.

I believe that no dominance methodology really stands up to scrutiny if your primary aim is a willing partner, either equine or canine (or human). When an animal shows aggressive behaviour in the wild, the other animals in the group will quietly choose to remove themselves from the aggressor's proximity. When humans use coercive or alpha-based training methods, the animal is never given the chance to remove himself from the unpleasant stimulus. Instead, the animal is subjected to ongoing dominance behaviour with no release or reprieve. What's natural about that? Round pen work, if you watch carefully, can often show stressed horses, running in circles with no chance of escape, demonstrating displacement behaviour and submission, rather than willing connection. Any situation where the horse is deprived of the choice to remove themselves from the pressure involves the use of an aversive mechanism. Strictly speaking, even the fence to a six acre field is an aversive, depriving the horse of choice. That's another difficult truth.

Conversely, the timing and tact required to use pressure

release, or request and reward, for meaningful two-way communication, whatever your methodology, is a skill that takes most people a lifetime to perfect. One of the most beautiful "dressage" riding sequences I have seen on film is the opening sequence to the film "Buck". Buck Brannaman is the original horse whisperer, on whom the world famous Nicholas Sparks novel and subsequent Robert Redford film, were based. Buck doesn't have a patented training system, or sell branded gadgets, although he has finally written some books. He is just a good old fashioned horseman who works with calm, common sense and a deep understanding and respect for his equine partner. In the opening sequence of the film, Buck is riding, no, dancing with his cutting horse, sashaying gracefully sideways in an open field. Horse and rider are in perfect mental and physical harmony, and the horse is in a lovely, efficient functional balance. The term Dressage actually derives from the French verb *dresser* — to train. So when we Do Dressage we are simply training our horses, to be the most beautiful and functional and efficient creatures they can be, improving in their balance and grace, even when hampered by us in the saddle.

And who wants total submission from their horse anyway? Modern cross country training ethos seems to rely on the fact that the horse will be more scared of the adverse consequences of not jumping the fence than he is of jumping the scary fence. How many sales adverts say Never stops? Personally, if I completely misjudge the correct stride on the approach to a fence, I would rather my horse save us both instead of turning himself inside out to take off and hopefully get to the other side. I want him to trust me so when things get scary he checks in with me — Are we OK? Are we going? What do we need to do? — before sorting us both out. I don't want him just to launch into the air in desperation.

Training classical dressage simply cannot be done by force. In early dressage training, we are incrementally teaching the horse to experiment with new and different ways of using their body; the reward is that the new muscle usage feels better and so the horse will spontaneously offer it again. This relaxed experimenting on the horse's part simply cannot occur in a coercive relationship. Successful classical training, similar to dance training, is the very antithesis of the dominance myth.

The classical reason for dressage training is to prepare the horse's body to be ridden. To the uneducated eye, horses look like incredibly powerful animals, with a back that begs to carry you off into the hills. In reality, that spine is more like a rope suspension bridge, hanging between shoulders and pelvis, with little natural support. If we simply sit on that rope bridge, in the nice convenient human sized dip, without first teaching the horse how to find an improved posture that allows them to carry us safely, all we do when riding them is cause damage to their backs.

I have spent many hours observing my horses in the field, while pulling ragwort and pooh picking and moving fencing and generally pottering around. They are three geldings, a bachelor gang, that have been together now for six years, mixed up with various short-term visitors. Paddy, the eldest, is twenty-four and Rocky is the youngest at eight. There really is no clear leader among them. They do all have different roles. Paddy is the sentinel. I cannot get within half a mile of them in any situation without him fixing his eyes on me and saying Hi! I have owned him the longest, and either the bond between us is very close, or his radar is very finely tuned. It is always Paddy that announces my presence to the herd.

Cal is very controlling about food. He really flexes his muscles and his teeth at meal times; I have always fed him first for ease and safety. This bolshy behaviour doesn't necessarily make the others want to hang out with him and often, if he was snoozing or if I took him out of the field to ride, the other two would spend the Cal-free time stuffing themselves at the haylage feeders. Cal is Irish born and bred, so I guess food may have been scarce at some point. That's resource guarding, not leadership.

Rocky still loves to play, mostly on two hind legs. Cal and Paddy take it in turns to entertain him, and to chastise him when he gets too annoying. No one in particular decides when to move, or when to drink, or when to go for a mosey to the vantage point; those decisions seem to occur organically and any one of the three horses can take the lead. When we had a little mare in with the boys, she did move them around a lot, I guess because she liked to prove that she could!

All these observations however are based on my horses, essentially in captivity. No matter how much I have enriched their field environment, it still has fenced boundaries, haylage feeders and limited grass when they were allowed on the middle; in other words, rationed resources. Lucy Rees, the ethologist, has studied horses extensively in the wild. She says, There's a lot of fiction written about wild horses. By that, she means that many of the books, and even scientific studies, describe horse behaviour in terms of dominance hierarchies, something which has never been observed in horses living under truly natural conditions. Yet these theories form the basis of many schools of horsemanship, even those purporting to be natural.

Her fascinating series of videos can be accessed for free on EponaTV, and should be required watching for all horse owners and horse lovers. In this video series, we meet the Pottoka ponies of the Gredos mountains in Northern Extremadura in Spain. The ponies lead a natural life in over a thousand hectares of wilderness. The purpose of the project is to study natural horse behaviour and also to keep the mountains clear of shrubs which can feed forest fires. Briefly: where there are adequate resources, and adequate space, there is no dominance behaviour demonstrated. The wild horses live in peaceful, co-operative family groups, and show collaborative, bonding behaviour and virtually no aggression.

There might be some posturing at breeding time, but there is no true conflict. Humans could learn a lot from horses.

In contrast, the seminal study that led to the myth of the alpha wolf was based on an observational study in the 1940s performed on wolves in captivity. Mech then published a book on the theory in the 1970s, which he has recently been trying to get withdrawn. A wolf pack in captivity, a bit like our domestic horses, is a group of disparate individuals who have been forcibly grouped together by their human owners, with no family relationship and scant regard for differing personalities. These individuals are then forced to compete for resources which are controlled and rationed by the humans. Funnily enough, the captive wolves fought a lot. The original study has since been compared to aliens learning about the behaviour of human families by observing people living in refugee camps.

So, if we are not to be the horse's alpha animal, what role can we assume? How about being their most trusted human? How about an equal relationship between two different species of animal based on mutual trust and affection? A dear friend describes good human-equine communication as tiptoeing up to the edge of the species divide. You cannot be the herd leader because you cannot be one of the herd. Believe me, these sentient and intelligent animals know you have two legs. They know you are other. Of course large animals need to understand physical boundaries, for everyone's safety, but we can set those parameters with energy and intent as well as very simple training — rewarding the behaviours we like and either not rewarding or discouraging the behaviours we don't like. Positive reinforcement does not have to involve treats; dogs and horses are first sentient: your approval and love is reward enough. (Although treats do help in the early days when puppies are super distractable.) I've used food as a distraction, for instance when clipping and trimming, but not as a specific positive reinforcement training aid. Horses are so good at understanding intent, they know when they have done well.

So please do your animals a favour. Look your horse or dog in the eye, softly, with eyebrows down, and try communicating with the smallest possible whispers or signals. Imagine you are in a war zone, or out hunting, and need to communicate with silent gestures and just a thought. Once you start to whisper, they will start to listen more closely. And once you observe them carefully, and try to praise rather than constantly saying, No, don't do that, you will be amazed at how they blossom.

It is not just our animals who suffer from this human obsession with a flawed paradigm. Imagine how much less stressful and more fun life at the office could be if we all worked together for the greater good rather than allowing behaviour that would not be out of place in a small shark tank! The world will be a much better place when we debunk this myth of the alpha.

Recommended Reading:

Rees, Lucy, *The Horses Mind,* Hutchinson (1993)

16

TAKE EVERY OPPORTUNITY TO PRAISE

Finding every opportunity to praise emphasises the power of positive feedback, and is the soundbite that epitomises my training philosophy.

I don't get too hung up on R+, R-. I do use so-called aversives like spurs and whips and bits, but I try to use them in the non-aversive way that we have been taught is possible by two thousand years of classical teaching. And I am willing to learn and evolve, with the horses as my most reliable and honest teachers.

So this chapter summarises where I am now. It's a long way from where I was ten years ago. And we may all read this in another ten years and think: what nonsense. I seek to share my current understanding because writing it down helps me to clarify my thoughts, and because occasionally it seems to help other people too.

In my teaching, and in life, I seek every opportunity to praise: the horse, the junior doctor, myself. It becomes a way of being: always seeking the opportunity to praise the positive in every action or interaction.

When Rocky, my glorious warmblood, was originally struggling with a sore back, he was still young, green and growing. My personal circumstances were a bit complicated at that time and so I made a conscious decision to take his rehab very slowly, to allow the growth spurt to complete, to let him down and let the spasmed muscles relax, to get him pain-free and in good shape physically and mentally and then to start again from the beginning.

I chose to pay meticulous attention to posture and correct muscle usage and to see if we could end up with a better back that would then allow me to sit on it without causing trouble or pain. This rationale also gave me the time to completely rebuild our training relationship from the ground, so that we could have trust and a good communication system in place before I got back on. This process set me thinking about how I train. I asked myself, very seriously — what is my methodology? And I arrived at my fundamental mantra: seek every opportunity to praise.

I have never tried full on formal clicker training. Currently, I don't own a horse that is more motivated by food than by praise, so the premise of training to a click backed up by a food reward doesn't work for my current equine partners. I'm also sure I would not be as quick to click as I am to praise with my voice, so for me it is much easier to mark with my voice. I guess that comes with prac-tise. But as horses are basically telepathic even if they don't hear the word, or the click, they hear the thought, so it seems to me the clicker just introduces a layer of delay. I'm also put off by the tragic story of Tilikum, the notorious killer whale at Sea World: when clicker training goes wrong, the result can be dangerous frustration for the animal and for the handler. I'm sure the horse will come along one day that forces me to learn clicker training and I will have to eat these words, as I have so many others! But life is a journey...

I have seen friends have very good results with clicker training and with pure R+ methods, without the need for the clicker itself. As with everything, there is no black or white, no right or wrong, we have to play to our strengths and learn what methods suit our animal's individual needs at a particular stage in our skills and our development.

The key question is what to praise. Now that the horses and I are back in company rather than living at home in our little private bubble, we are once again exposed to other humans and their relationships with their horses.

One can learn a lot by listening. The other day a livery neighbour was grooming her pony. Every other word seemed to be a No, or a Don't Do That, or a Stop That, or another No. How do we get into that habit? When we dreamed of having horses, or dogs, or maybe even children, did we dream of telling them off the whole time? I am a proud survivor of surgical training: in the good old days, you knew you were doing well if the boss kept quiet, and you only got spoken to, or rapped on the knuckles, if you were doing it wrong. When we read about how to raise children, the experts tell us that the average toddler hears the word No an astonishing four hundred times a day. That's not only tiresome for you; it can also be harmful to your child: According to studies, kids who hear No too much have poorer language skills than children whose parents offer more positive feedback.

But if we just randomly say Good Boy, how will the horse, or the child, learn what was good or desired? I have found that it's all about timing.

Here's an example. Rocky, the young warmblood, has really mobile shoulders and very expressive front legs. His reaction to food, to buckets, to grooming, to challenge, is to wave his right foreleg around, and because he is tall and I am average, for me the waving is often at waist height. There is no point telling him not to do this; by the time I am saying No Don't Do That the foot is already up in the air. He doesn't choose to do it, it's a reaction, an instinct. Horses don't reason or plan, they react. There is no possible way of teaching the horse Don't Do That once the action has already occurred.

Instead, how about teaching him to put the leg back down on the ground on command? At first this is opportunistic training; every time the leg hits the ground as he's scraping or waving, I praise – Down. Good. Eventually, I just have to say Down and the leg will land. I don't want to teach him not to wave the leg around. Who knows, I might want him to do the flamboyant Spanish Walk one day, although I'm not sure that his body will ever need that particular exercise as his shoulders are already mobile enough. So the principle of positive feedback is this: rather than using a negative admonishment after the unwanted behaviour has occurred, instead teach a positive correction to the unwanted behaviour, a correction that we can first cue and then reward.

This has the advantage of not eliminating a behaviour or movement we may want to access again in the future, and it also gives us the opportunity to praise our horse rather than rebuke him. Horses, like children, like dogs, respond much better to positive feedback than negative. They enjoy being right, and being rewarded for being right.

Another common misconception is that we can get a horse to calm down by stroking or patting them when they are on high alert. Effectively, what we are doing here is rewarding the horse for being anxious or fractious. Assuming they even register the so-called soothing touch, it is often delivered by a human with a matching high heart rate and a suddenly anxious and squeaky voice. Once you the human are acting from your fearful demeanour, the horse's concern is justified. Harmonising with the anxiety or failing to change the mood is reinforcement. Instead the horse should be allowed time to process the alarming stimulus in a calm manner, facilitated by a neutral and non-threatening human. I am sure we humans totally underestimate the horse's ability to learn from positive experience. Far better to change the mood and then reward the following calm processing, which is the desired behaviour.

How do we change the mood? Laughter or yawning are my two favourite strategies here. When Cal was a youngster and we were hacking around Kingsley as the annual scarecrow competition hit full swing, I just had to giggle at the crazy stuff in the hedges. The best one was a pair of legs, sticking up out of the hedge, as if diving into a pool. (I think it must have been Commonwealth Games year.) Cal would be eyeballing the scarecrows and sidling past at speed and I would be chuckling and giggling, but with hands loose on the reins and concentrating on loose legs and relaxed seat. He's pretty cool about most stuff now.

At competitions with Cal, or handling Rocky recently when he's been in pain having physio, I focus on relaxation and yawning. Relaxed breathing slows your heart rate and lowers your energy, while yawning relaxes the jaw and the neck, and therefore the hands, as well as changing the frequency of your thoughts. When the horse comes down in energy, relaxes or yawns, then we can take the opportunity to praise the relaxation and the calm, because that is the desired behaviour.

The other trick here is to change the balance. Horses are kinaesthetic — by which I mean their mood and their body state are innately connected. Being out of balance unnerves them. Conversely being in balance is empowering. So if we can balance them in a moment of alarm, help connect the brain back to both hind legs, they will become calmer. How we do that is with a relatively simple technique; move the shoulders around the hind legs to line up weight of head and neck with the inside hind leg, connect this to the outside rein, back them up a few strides to shift the weight back. Ensuring that both hind legs are equally loaded and evenly supporting the horse's weight has a very calming effect on the horse's brain.

Now please don't get me wrong here, I'm know I'm far from perfect. I'm not trying to preach, just to share some stuff I have learned. The night I first wrote this was worming night, and Rocky still had me swinging around the stable because yet again I hadn't done enough preparatory work in between worming doses. But it reminded me I need to do that prep work, and it will get easier. Aside — 6 months of ulcer treatment later, he now comes to the front of the stable clearing out his mouth with his tongue ready for the antacid paste). When I'm riding nowadays, I'm always looking for the moment to praise, the neck and top-line stretch or the moment of power coming through, or relaxation that I can mark as desirable so that I will be offered it again. I am also careful to praise myself — although that's much more subtle. I don't vocalise any of those moments so much, although maybe I should, but a turn in balance or good use of a seat aid will get noted as a nice feeling, or a good moment, with a nod or a smile.

More importantly, I don't beat myself up for the not perfect moments any more. I have a giggle, regroup and do it again, better. I no longer hate my disobedient legs, or my flappy elbow, or my gripping left hand. Instead I notice them, change them, forgive myself, correct them again, until the corrections become fewer and further between. And then you notice your flappy knee or your sticky out toe and move on to the next bit of homework. Finding every opportunity to praise, both ourselves and our horses, keeps training fun and rewarding, and beats the winter blues.

Here's some homework for your pause for thought:

- First: spend an evening with your horse, or your dog, or your child, or even your lover, just listening to what you say to them. Is it no or is it yes, is it don't do that or clever.
- Next: spend an evening being really careful to look for the moment to praise, both you and them, for the good stuff, and to replace a Don't with a Can you do this instead?
- And then observe both your moods.
- I predict your partner will be proud and puffed up and loving at the end of a positive session. And you will be energised and enthused and looking forward to the next session, no matter what has occurred, because you have both had more fun. And the sudden improvement might happen over a very long time, because there is pure magic in the power of perfectly-timed positive feedback.

Recommended Reading:

Rees, Lucy, *Horses in Company*, JA Allen (2017)

Thiel, Ulrik E, *Ridden: Dressage from the Horse's Point of View*, Trafalgar Square Books (2013)

17

FIRST DO NO HARM

I am a surgeon in my other life, so first do no harm is the mantra that I live by, day to day. I try to apply it in every interaction in my life: human to human, and human to horse.

I truly believe that we all love our horses and we work really hard for them and with them, and nobody that got into horses ever did so with the intention of causing harm. But here is an awkward truth:

The intention to harm need not be present for harm to occur.

So, how might we harm our horses? The first, most obvious example is by causing the horse to bleed. We may have different standards but surely we can agree that, as a basic principle, nothing that I do to my beloved horse should make him or her bleed. I can't claim that I have never caused a horse to bleed; once upon a time, when Paddy was in work, I rubbed his side raw in a jumping lesson, not even with a spur but with the spur rest from my boot. Yes, he does have incredibly thin skin. But that wasn't an excuse. I rubbed his side raw because my leg position wasn't good enough in those days and I was gripping with my calves, in that knees out, heels jammed in, stable, secure and incorrect position that jumping trainers encourage because being wedged in increases the security of the novice rider in the saddle.

It wouldn't happen now. After four years and hundreds of hours of lessons and homework, my leg position has changed entirely, my seat is now more balanced and secure and I no longer need to grip with my calves. I mostly aid with the inside of my foot, not the heel or the back of my calf. I still blob off occasionally though!

When Cal was a youngster I rubbed his soft, fleshy lips raw with the bit. The well-meaning livery yard owner gave me some crystals to mix with water to harden up his mouth. I was an idiot and uneducated and I used the solution and carried on schooling. No one suggested I should learn to use the bit better or learn to keep my hands still (the importance of that independent seat again). No, it was the young horse's soft mouth that was the problem and there was a caustic solution for that. Rocky has not had a sore mouth. Now I have learned that the bit should only act up or out, never backwards and never down on the bars or the tongue, that the length of rein is dictated by the horse, that the horse's frame dictates the length of rein and the horse's level of balance and schooling dictates the frame. And I have a more secure seat that allows me to think forwards with my hands without losing balance. Obviously I'm still nowhere near perfect, but I'm learning and striving to be better all the time. And if I caused one of my horses to bleed in a competition I would eliminate myself and kick myself and run for home to train and improve myself so it could never happen again.

There are other more insidious ways of causing harm to a horse. The modern fashion of riding dressage horses Low, Deep and Round, or LDR, with their head and necks well behind the vertical — also given kind sounding names like deep stretching, or yoga for horses — has been shown by more than fifty scientific studies (summarised by the ISES) to be both physically and mentally damaging for the horse. Modern science is now proving what the Old Dead Guys already knew by keen observation — that closed postures and curling the front of the horse for show, rather than riding from behind seeking weighted and flexed haunches for correct biomechanics, lead to problems with kissing spines, suspensory ligament pathology, joint damage, and hock arthritis. Being ridden out of balance also contributes to mental stress and gastric ulcers. Pulling horses' heads in and down limits their field of vision, and then they develop stress from learned helplessness. Please don't take my word for it; read the extensive research and then make your own minds up.

But do remember: To know and not to do is not to know. We are naturally quick to criticise others, and all of us are just doing our best. How will we know if the work we are doing is correct? Luckily, horses are very clear communicators once we have learned to look and listen. I've altered the quote below, from Maya Angelou: I have learned that horses will forget what you said, horses will forget what you do, but horses will never forget how you made them feel.

How can we know that our work is good? In a world where so much teaching is against the horse rather than for the good of the horse, how will we tell the difference? After all, the whole point of dressage — from the French verb *dresser* which actually means to train — is to sculpt our horse into a thing of beauty, a creature that is empowered rather than diminished by our interventions.

How do we know whether the work made his body feel better? What signs do we look for to know that our work made the horse feel good? My favourite sign is helicopter ears, ones that go soft and floppy and assume all sorts of funny angles. Rocky has huge ears, as do the rest of his family, so this one is pretty obvious, as well as being visible from on top. Another sign is soft liquid eyes, with relaxed eyebrows and slow blinking. When the work is good, the horse is calm, because horses are kinaesthetic and they find it frightening to be out of balance. When their balance is aided in a way that improves their posture, they relax and chill out. They almost look stoned after good work. Stoned, not exhausted. Breathing slows and calms: soft hurrumphs or gentle chuntering are signs of a relaxed mouth, tongue and larynx as well as relaxed brain. Harsh sharp breathing, breath holding, or sharp snorting, teeth grinding or calling out are all sure signs of a horse either stressed or on full alert.

> In the French Tradition, it is the state of the mouth that governs everything. There are three mouths possible. A dry mouth, a soaking wet one with gobs of foam on the chest and legs, and a moist one in which the lips are just moist and the lower jaw relaxed. The third mouth is described as being *fraiche* and offers a gentle murmur (L'Hotte) as if to be smiling (Beudant). It is to this third mouth that we should aspire.

This is a quote from James Sandy Dunlop, a retired orthopaedic surgeon who has enjoyed a special interest in the French School of academic horsemanship for the last 35 years.

I always get off the horse after a work session and look critically at the muscles. Is the neck soft and inflated, are the under neck muscles soft, does the neck come nicely out of the shoulder girdle? Does it look wider at the base than the middle or the top? A good neck should be an even triangle from withers to poll, and from shoulder girdle to poll. The horses that are ridden extensively in the damaging LDR posture have this weird tube of muscle that runs up from the middle of their necks, with no splenius or trapezius. In layman's terms they have a hollow missing triangle just in front of the withers and also under the pommel. Is the lumbar back full? Does the horse's skin shine and glisten and move smoothly over his frame or does it look dry and tight and stuck to the bones?

Is the tail carried, or clamped tightly? Does it swing softly as he moves? If the tail swings, the back can't be braced.

And finally, does the horse look proud after work? Does he go strutting back to the field to tell his mates how cool he was? Does he look better and stronger and bigger each time? Does he offer the improved posture next ride without you having to do the prep work? If he offers the new posture or the new body usage next time, you know that the change felt good and he's choosing to seek that posture. If you have to do all the work all over again, every time, then it didn't feel better for him. And that means it probably wasn't right. In which case, don't repeat it. Because as Charles de Kunffy famously said if you aren't improving your horse you are breaking him down. And, as I might have mentioned before, our first responsibility is to do no harm.

Further Reading:

Karl, Philippe, *Twisted Truths of Modern Dressage: a Search for a Classical Alternative,* Cadmos Verlag (2008)

Heuschmann, Gerd, *Balancing Act: The Horse in Sport— An Irreconcilable Conflict?,* Trafalgar Square Books (2021)

18

THE ROCKY ROAD TO REHAB

It took me many weeks of self-recrimination and analysis before I was able to write about my glorious youngster's diagnosis of back problems and his subsequent road to rehabilitation. I know all about the joys of rehab: it has been seven years since Cal fractured his carpal bone. And I completely believe a good outcome is possible. Cal's fracture taught me to trust the process and detach from the outcome. He has become the most fabulous horse you could wish for, and the fracture, although well healed, ensured that he became another horse I could never sell.

I'm not sure how anyone manages to sell horses.

I remember every step of the rehab rollercoaster; the early uncertainty, the agony of box rest, the hundreds of miles we walked in hand, and then finally the relief when he jumped his first round of show jumps and stayed sound.

I had never expected to be on the road to rehab with Rocky. He came to me as a yearling, well bred, well handled, but completely unspoilt, from a trusted source. He came from the South Coast, collected on a crazy road trip for a three-day event at Longleat Safari Park, where Paddy dropped me in a ditch full of wooden crocodiles. Paddy did share some wise words with Rocky on the trip home though: the youngster travelled like a pro and learned to eat out of a haynet on the way.

We turned him out with another colt at a friend's place and let them be boys, living out and razzing around together. He came in to the livery yard aged three, a couple of months before the big move to the field on the edge of the forest. Once the land was sorted the three horses went out together full time and gelled as a little herd straight away.

The reason for the full-on pity party has its roots in my belief system. Everything I have learned over the last few years, the entire focus of my equine learning, has been about correct classical training, training that is meant to preserve the health of the horse and prevent this type of injury.

Good work is meant to be therapeutic. Rehab is really just about going back to absolute basics, working on the ground, opening up those intervertebral spaces between the spinous processes that stick up like Stegosaurus spikes in horses' backs, and building the muscle in between. It's basically what we should be doing all along. Rocky had the troublesome intervertebral joint space medicated, and this was followed up with some ultrasound to the muscles of his lumbar region, and a few weeks of muscle relaxant medication, as these muscles were in spasm.

The ODGs (Old Dead Guys) knew all about kissing spines, or spinal process crowding syndrome; correct classical training focuses on opening the back, elongating the top line, thereby preventing this problem from occurring. Piaffe, a sort of trot on the spot, is the ultimate test of collection and actually, when done correctly, shows an increase in length from tail to poll along the arch of the top line. All good piaffe should then be able to lift into a levade. The levade involves the horse standing in balance on the hind legs and requires even more length of topline, as well as huge strength in the quarters. The lumbar back is curved, the loins coiled, the hind legs and hocks flexed.

I have always taken Rocky's work really slowly. He did six weeks of in hand work and was sat on briefly at the age of three. He then did about three more months of in hand work and was ridden away for six weeks at four. Then, in his fifth summer, he did a few fun rides, a bit of light schooling and hacking, and a bit of pole-work. In his sixth year, the work was meant to get a bit more consistent.

This is not a young horse that has been over-worked. Or was he? As often happens, human working lives have been the limiting factor, as well as Rocky's so-called tricky nature. Do we even believe horses can have tricky natures? I was starting to use judgmental words about him. I called him backwards. I told myself he had the work ethic of a flea because he would stop dead when tired and have a little buck when asked to go forwards. I should have known better.

So the pity party was all about where I had got it all wrong. Had I done too much work with him too young? Had I ridden him too much, when we should have been building a stronger horse with good in hand work and just riding a little? Or was the injury the result of an unfortunate conformational glitch? Did the injury occur when he got stuck under the partition in the truck a couple of years ago? He didn't thrash around or panic but still...

And then, after a couple of days of madness, I gave myself a slap and a talking to. It doesn't matter how it happened. I just needed to focus on the rehabilitation journey.

Rehabilitation is a wild ride of emotions, hopes and dreams, when actually one should just knuckle down, do the work and trust the process. All of the previous learning, all of the work on posture, timing, training, helping horses find biomechanically correct movement, would surely come into play even more now. The value of good in hand work cannot be overstated. I never manage to do as much as I should. Only last week, Cal, my supposedly advanced horse, was the demo pony for a training clinic, which meant I was the demo human (gulp). We found a few holes in the simple work — for example, the shoulder in left, meant to be a beautiful flowing sideways movement, has too much neck bend, and so doesn't weight the inside hind leg or develop good stretch along the outside of the horse. And in leg yield left, a side stepping movement meant to develop flexibility, he doesn't actually choose to step past his barrel with his hind leg. The mistakes are much easier to feel and correct from the ground if we are observant and honest enough with ourselves.

Some vets recommend a training aid when rehabbing a horse with kissing spines. These so-called training aids are various arrangements of ropes and pulleys that hold or limit the horse to a certain position or posture while the human lunges them in circles. The advantages are supposedly that it stretches the horse over the back. Over the back is a horrid modern phrase that has no true biomechanical meaning and does not actually describe any desirable attribute according to the classical training literature.

Let's take a slight detour into classical equestrian literature and its' relevance to the modern rider, as well as to the rehab horse. There is a vast body of historical literature, detailing two thousand years of classical training methods. In days of old, horses were a serious lifetime investment, not a plaything or a commodity. They were bought to last. For the medieval knight, the *chevalier*, the *caballero*, all names which literally mean the horseman, the horse was their main asset, their livelihood as well as part of their job description, reputation and identity. In mounted combat, the horsemen's lives literally depended on having a powerful, well-trained and willing horse. The horse and the rider had to trust each other, to work together, and to fight together. Longevity in their horses was very important to these horsemen. Training a horse to peak performance for armed combat at close quarters takes a long time. The horse needs to build power and strength as well as learn the manoeuvres; it is only logical that the training described in the historical writings was developed for maximum soundness and preservation of the horse as well as for nailing those badass war horse moves.

The disadvantages of the rope and pulley family of training aids are that anything restrictive attached to the metal bit placed in the horse's mouth only serves to teach the horse to avoid pressure from the bit. (Imagine jagging yourself in the teeth every time you move a leg. You would not move forward with a song in your heart if that happened.) I repeat: the bit action is meant as an aid to assist communication, not an aversive tool of control or restriction.

When I lunge, in accordance with the centuries of teaching, all influence on the head is from the human hand to the front of the lungeing cavesson. The cavesson is a special piece of headgear that looks like a bridle but is designed to be super stable on the head as the horse is worked in long lines, either on a circle or from behind. The lines are attached to metal rings on the noseband of the cavesson. Lungeing and long lining is a very specific skill set in the art of classical horse training. Used well, the horse is encouraged to reach forwards, which teaches the horse to stretch and balance all through its body and develop the back muscles that make up the all important topline that will one day support both the rider and the horse. The feeling of connection to the cavesson should be like the feeling down the rein when ridden, and the lunge lines held exactly like a rein in the hand.

Like everything else in riding, the hand hold on the rein has a very precise correct position based on sound biomechanical principles. The leather rein is held in the upright hand. The upright position of the hand is very important because, at this angle, the two long bones of the human forearm are lined up in a neutral position so the muscles of the arm can act in an elastic way without being blocked by any twist in the forearm bones. The upper arm hangs vertically down from the shoulder and becomes part of the long back muscles. The point of most pressure on the reins is between the bent thumb pressing down on the first bone of the index finger. This activates the triceps muscle in the back of the upper arm. In this way, the upper arm, is connected to the back, which is connected to the seat bone, and tiny movements of the shoulder blades can be felt by the horse in the riders "seat". Now do you get an inkling of why the tiny details matter?

The hand may only act forward, up, and out, and we continually place the point of contact in front of the horse so that he learns to reach forwards to find again the point of contact that acts as reference for balance. There is no restriction or backward pulling action in this work, just as in classical tradition there should never be any backward or restrictive action on the bit. This is the feeling we then translate to the bit when we move on to the next stage of training.

In classical tradition, the bit belongs to the horse. The metal bit that we place in the horse's mouth should be used as a tool to aid subtle communication. It is not an instrument of control or coercion. The bit should never be used against the horse, neither as a crude means of control nor as a leverage tool to round the neck. Because we place this piece of metal in the horse's mouth, we have a duty to make sure the bit fits, first in width, but also that the shape of the mouthpiece conforms to the shape of the horse's lips, palate and tongue. Lorinery, the ancient art of bitting, is a complex craft that we have woefully neglected in recent times.

We also have a responsibility as riders to learn how to use the bit correctly, to develop an independent seat and educate our hands. Even the subtlest of left/right actions backwards on the bars of the mouth or downwards on the tongue teaches the horse to avoid the aversive (unpleasant) pressure and duck behind the bit to relieve the pain. The horse has to learn to trust the bit, to take it forwards, to use it as a point of reference to reach towards and work around, just like the barre acts as a point of reference or balance for the advanced ballerina. The novice ballerina may use the barre for occasional balance, but as she becomes stronger and more accomplished, the barre no longer needs to be held or gripped. In the same way, the advanced horse uses the bit as a point of balance.

The old medieval curbs look barbaric to our uneducated eyes, but the long shanks actually allow a much greater degree of finesse due to the laws of leverage. With a long shank in a well balanced bit, the curb chain that runs under the chin is then activated by the lightest touch. When an advanced horse that has been trained in truly correct classical tradition is working in a curb, that horse isn't responding to bit pressure at all but to the curb chain or strap tickling the vibrissae or sensory whiskers that grow under the horses' chin. Like a cat, the horse's whiskers are fully equipped sensory organs, each with its own individual nerve. So a curb bit used well is a means of achieving complex and delicate communication, in whispers, a hair's breadth. We don't see them used like that very much in our modern FEI competition world.

There are some gadgets or training aids that have no direct restrictive influence on the front end of the horse. I have been using stretchy therapy bands that go loosely under the tummy and around the back of the hocks, to encourage Rocky to lift his tummy and round his back. One could also use just the back part of some of the more famous training aids. The important point is that these gadgets should be used as aids to proprioception, not tightened up to work in a restrictive way that physically limits the range of movement. We want the horse to experiment with different muscle patterns and learn that good movement feels better.

In hand work also teaches us about our horse's training brain. Rocky has always thrown his whole genetically-gifted body at any task. When I ask him to slow down and actually work within himself, paying attention to the details of which leg goes where, he then needs to work really slowly, with lots of breathing and thinking breaks. This is timing and observation I will need to take forward to the ridden work once we get back on.

It's also important not to pussyfoot around with the rehab horse, or with any horse. We mustn't continually look at them as if they are broken. Horses, as prey animals, find this really disconcerting. The broken horse becomes lunch for the lion. Instead, we should look at them with soft eyes, taking in the details of the movement: the stretch needed here, the balance needed there. We should do all the best work, asking nothing less than enough, yet noticing and rewarding every try that gets us towards better. Horses on full throttle are magnificent beasts, yet so much of what we do as humans actually diminishes them to our level so that we can use them within our comfort zone. We want them to be calm and soft, and with us, yet with their full power either in use or instantly available. We should remind them of their magnificence, encourage them to use themselves fully and correctly, and welcome the moment when the whole, fabulous horse turns up.

Perhaps most importantly on the Rocky road to rehab, we should never underestimate the healing power of love, positive energy, and sunshine.

Further resources and reading:

Horse Bit Fit have consultants all over the UK and do a great online course for owners as well as an advanced course for practitioners overseas:
www.Horsebitfit.com

Robichon de la Gueriniere, Francois, *School of Horsemanship,* translated by Boucher, Tracy, JA Allen (1993)

Ritter, Thomas, *The Biomechanical Basics of Classical Riding,* Cadmos (2011)

De Kunffy, Charles, *The Athletic Development of the Dressage Horse,* Howell reference Books (1992)

19

IF ONLY MY HORSE COULD TALK

How many times have we all said those words? In jest, or in despair? But what if our horses are equally frustrated, stamping their feet and tossing their manes and screaming, If only my human would listen!

They don't actually scream of course. Horses are the masters of subtlety — until the situation gets really bad and then they need to get really loud. Amongst themselves horses talk mostly in whispers: a sideways look, a flick of an ear, an imperceptible yield. Horses are naturally very peaceable animals. I have previously mentioned the equine ethologist, Lucy Rees, who has spent much of her life observing horses in the wild. She writes,

> To understand horses and their difficulties in our hands, we need to watch them as they really are, without anthropomorphic interpretations and expectations.

These lifelong studies are beautifully summarised in her latest offering, *Horses In Company* (2017), a book whose evolutionary perspective revolutionises our view of horse society.

For me, her most astonishing finding is that, in an environment in which there is no resource shortage, horses exhibit virtually no conflict behaviour. I have written about this before, when I dissected the context of that other myth, the alpha male. This lesson is one that I thought I had learned already. But as the saying goes: until you truly know something, and take that truth to heart and actually act on that truth, you don't really know.

The last year and a half have been really tricky for me and Rocky, due to his diagnosis of a sore back due to kissing spines. His initial time off and then six months of slow and careful rehabilitation coincided with my change in personal circumstances. However, as we got back into consistent work there was no real improvement to his tricky behaviour. His back looked and felt perfect, with improving muscle coverage and no sore spots, but his behaviour remained erratic. I was still getting regular reminders on the inevitable force of gravity.

I had arranged for the vets to endoscope him for gastric ulcers a couple of years ago, at the beginning of his working life. The rationale then was partly to check out his behaviour, but was mainly based on the fact that at the time he was a full hundred kilos lighter than his two equally classy sisters. That first scope was essentially clear. The vets had looked at me with sceptical eyebrows when I explained my reasons for scoping him: he is plenty big enough and a strapping lad and he didn't look poor or unhealthy at the time. However, I was the client and it was my money to spend as I wished.

It turned out that he had some very mild traces of inflammation, but no true ulceration. The vets didn't push me to treat him formally at that time and were quite happy when I said I would organise an empirical trial of treatment with the generic version of Omeprazole that one can buy online. He did put a good amount of weight on, so I thought he must be better, and we never repeated the scope. And his behaviour never changed. He was still occasionally obstreperous but nothing, I told myself, that one wouldn't expect or excuse from a young horse.

On the ground he is the sweetest, most affectionate horse you could imagine. He just loves people and adores a good fuss. I call him the Labra-dude. Because he had previously been scoped clear, with no behavioural benefit following on from that trial of treatment (isn't the retrospect-oscope a wonderful instrument?), the possibility of ongoing ulcers just didn't enter my brain. I am a very literal thinker, and my brain really only works in lists and straight lines so, in my head, ulcers were ticked off, as was back trouble. All that was left was learned behaviour and an athletic, sharp and strong-minded horse that I had to decide if I was capable of riding.

Rocky has the most beautiful paces I have ever sat on. Had I not bought him as a youngster, I would never have been able to afford his Olympic standard genetics. For those of you who are into bloodlines, he is by Royaldik. Heraldik is a very well known sire to all eventing fans. Ingrid Klimke's Butts Abraxas, Andreas Dibowski's Butts Leon, and Sam Griffith's Happy Times are all Olympic eventers among the top flight horses sired by Heraldik. At the World Equestrian Games in 2010, Heraldik had three offspring in the Eventing and two in the Show Jumping.

Heraldik had a full sister called Herka, and Royaldik is out of Herka. And Royaldik's full brother Rohdiamant is also rated the World Number Three dressage stallion. Put simply, my gorgeous little baby Rocky is literally the most well-bred horse I am ever likely to own. Particularly as his famous relatives have proved to be functional as well as flash, with the confirmation to withstand a busy life at top level competition.

I remember vividly teaching Cal to jump. Until he learned to canter and developed the bulk of muscle required to carry his draught bone along the ground, let alone get it up in the air, jumping an eighty centimetre parallel always felt like a lottery. By contrast, Rocky can be looking at everything else, going sideways, and then just pop the same fence as a minor inconvenience as it appears in his path. All of which is a very long-winded way of saying I wasn't going to give up on that feeling without a fight. It's addictive, sitting on a horse that gives you a feeling of such ease over a fence. It's not quite so addictive hitting the ground on a regular basis.

As I tell this story now the answer is so fricking obvious that I am cringing as I type these words. I share this story, as brutally and as honestly as I can, to help you avoid similar obstinate mistakes, and to spare your horse having to shout at you quite so loudly. Rocky had severe separation anxiety. He was dramatically reactive to all new situations, to horses coming up behind us, to getting a bit too far away from other horses, to a gate closing. He would freeze out on hacks, at invisible obstacles. His reaction to any unexpected stimulus was to dump me and run.

He had been scoped for ulcers. His back was now fine. We had checked the saddle situation and solved it with a gorgeous Stride Free Jump. So I decided we needed remedial training. My long-term jumping instructor helped me with the riding and the training and we lunged him thoroughly before we got on to establish forwards. We taught him that forwards was required before all else.

And he did become more rideable. I gave it my best shot. I rode him five days a week, every week, all winter, through the dark and the cold and the rain. I even sent my beloved Cal away on loan so I had the time to concentrate on Rocky. We had regular lessons and training outings. And he did come on really well. He put on muscle, his back improved, his canter got stronger. But he still bucked.

One week in January, he put me on the floor three times in the same week. And there were no mitigating factors. He had done enough work, there were no scary things out there, I was riding at my usual time, in my normal routine. The same week he booted our lovely livery yard groom in the chest and shook her up really badly. And I just knew I couldn't do it any more. I couldn't keep putting myself through it, and we couldn't keep him safely here. I had got to a point where I couldn't steel myself to sit on him any more. I searched my heart and I made arrangements for him to go on sales livery. I was absolutely at peace with that decision. I think a few of my friends were even quite relieved.

I had a couple of weeks to spare before he could go, and my long-term mentor and classical dressage instructor suggested I scope him once more. It made sense. I couldn't conscientiously sell a sick horse, and I would be gutted if I sold my horse of a lifetime because he was too quirky for me and then found out someone else had treated him for something so simple and he turned out to be a poppet under saddle as well as on the ground.

Of course, when he was scoped it turned out that he had ulcers. Really bad ulcers. Multiple lesions, grade three ulcers, lots of grade two, significant amounts of fibrin deposits and areas of irritation. OK, I thought, I'll treat him, but he's still going. Once he's healed, he's still for sale. Then Corona came along and lockdown happened, about two weeks into his ulcer treatment. He's not a horse you could leave out of work altogether, his brain is quite active and he does find mischief. So I had to get back on and ride him, just light hacking, in company, to keep him ticking over and his brain occupied. Nothing too challenging....

He just got better, and better. The bucking objections turned into leg flicks and stalls, then to little ear flicks. He was safe to hack out on his own, with no trouble at previously nappy corners. We could cross the main road (a major barrier previously) and go around the whole village. We had to stop occasionally and check out things like a scarf left on a street sign, but he looked and worked it out whereas before he would have dumped me and run away. We even did the long circuit under the railway bridges and went past the scary white log on the bridle path on our own, after a few looks and a couple of reverses. But they were only reverses, not gymnastics. And I could feel his brain working it all out rather than his body reacting.

I'm still an idiot. And we were still in lockdown. As we couldn't do the second check scope at the time I let his meds run down to see what would happen. About a week after the PPI ran out and the day after the Misoprostol finished, I swung my leg into the saddle and instantly felt like I was sitting on a different horse.

I had to prove it, of course. I am still an idiot. He dropped me in the school, but I doggedly got back on and we went around the block. It was tense but manageable. Until we got back inside the gate, and then he tried to drop me on the concrete.

So we started the medication again. It took a few weeks to get back to lovely horse again. But he had been very clear, and yes, the lesson obviously needed reiterating. My horse doesn't have behaviour problems. He has pain problems. I am genuinely ashamed that he had to get to a point of shouting out his pain so loudly at me that I put both of us in danger.

As I write this, Rocky has just been scoped again. The ulcers look much better. We are still only on light work but he is putting on huge amounts of muscle. He is currently off the transfer list!

So, the key question: how much of bad horse behaviour is actually pain?

If only my human could listen.

20

THE UNBEATABLE LIGHTNESS OF BEING

There is an unbeatable lightness of being that we can achieve with our horses. For me, this is the ultimate goal of all riding and training. Once you have felt this lightness of bearing, this poetry in motion, it becomes addictive, and nothing less will do.

I still hold and cherish the vivid memories of my initiation into these glorious moments. The gait was canter, and the arena exercise was three strides of a slight sideways feeling in shoulder fore, straighten the horse onto the diagonal line for three strides, then plié sideways back to the fence for three strides, and repeat. The difficulty of the exercise was relatively high for us at that time. Our execution was far from perfect, but the result of the exercise was to create the most incredible war horse underneath me. If I close my eyes and go back there I can still feel Cal-tastic, all puffed up with smooth inflated muscle, underneath but mostly up and in front of me, his shoulder apparatus maximum width, his withers lifting me up, his neck huge, up and out in front of me, like a fighting dragon. The rein connection to the bit felt light yet firm in my hands, and he felt completely balanced between my hand and my seat. His footfalls were almost silent. In that moment, I could have put him anywhere in the arena, speared my enemy with a lance, jumped an enormous hedge, asked for a flying change, or halted him into a levade, if I had those skills. He was completely engaged, completely available, completely on it and completely with me. That is my current best description of lightness in riding, that lightness of being.

It was a surprise, because there was nothing soft about it. My previous horse, Paddy, the now-retired grandee, had been extensively ridden behind the vertical in his early education, and then by me before I knew any better. I had mistakenly associated his customary hiding behind the bit with lightness. Of course an empty hand feels soft and kind, but actually that emptiness is the opposite of contact: the horse is curling behind the vertical to avoid painful pressure on the delicate tongue.

This contact I felt with Cal was more tangible. He really filled my hand. There was a true connection, like linking arms on a summer's day. There was nothing restrictive about it, but there was a definite sensation of holding something precious, something that must not be dropped.

And it was about much more than the hand; my seat was filled with my horse's back, wide and firm but comfortable and malleable. My back was straight, my legs stable. It felt like sitting on firm memory foam, totally cushioned and supported, but active as well. In dressage language, I felt that I had an adhesive seat on an inflated back.

The beauty only lasted for a few strides of course; in training at our level these perfect moments are still fleeting. But that brief glimpse was enough to know that I would seek that feeling, every day, in every ride, until that becomes our normal way of going. Had we been in a double bridle, we would have been on a loose curb, because, in that moment, he filled the rein. It wasn't me chasing or seeking contact with him.

I have felt it a few times since. The last time it occurred we got our first clean canter to walk transition. I'm still amazed at how much power the horse requires to achieve lightness. Cal the daft draught is quite soporific to ride; his mind is hugely powerful and he's perfectly happy working on low revs. I call him the hypnotist: I get on him full of the best intentions, determined to access the whole amazing war horse body — and get off having had a lovely nice ride!! For him to be fully light, he needs to be fully engaged, brain, body and soul. He doesn't yield (or step up?) to that easily. Therein lies our biggest homework. When he does turn up he is huge, in body and in personality. He and I aren't always comfortable with that.

Lightness in riding is surely the ultimate goal, the magic we all seek, whatever our level. To be body to body and heartbeat to heartbeat with this magnificent creature, surely that is the fundamental reason we all ride. The demonstration of the highest pinnacle of training at the Spanish Riding School is the solo display. The rider holds the birch switch upright in one hand, the snaffle reins hang loose, and the curb reins are held lightly in the other hand. The solo display would typically include all the Grand Prix movements and finish with piaffe to levade, without a single aid being visible: horse and rider as one, effortless centaurs, mind and body melded, in the unbeatable lightness of being.

How do we get there? For the non-rider, there are other equivalents. The elite athletes call these moments being in the flow. I have felt it rock climbing, another form of dancing, the perfection of pulling through a move that looked implausible, as feet push and arms strain and tendons scream and all the while the heart is slow and the breathing centred, as you pull down and rise again. Or snow dancing, putting down a perfect set of tracks in powder, knees popping, thighs burning, floating on the edge of control. Or cloud dancing, scrambling and skipping along the ridge of Crib Goch, above the cloud inversion on a clear winter's day, the

Snowdon Horseshoe spread before you, smoke from friends' houses hanging tangy in the air.

Or the nearest feeling to pure flow, on those rare days when running is easy, when legs and heart and arms and lungs all pump in time, when the ground falls away and trees glide past, when effort becomes meditation and every fibre of your being resonates with your heartbeat. That is the closest feeling to dancing in tune with the world. Now, imagine that in tune with your horse.

For the equestrian to achieve this feeling, first we have to look to our own body before we can meld with another. We need a good seat, the seat that in the old days would have been developed over years of lessons on the lunge, the instructor controlling the horse and barking out orders for exercises that develop balance, and an adhesive seat with a supple back and allowing joints, with each leg and each arm able to act independently, in several parts, so that eventually we can aid each footfall if required.

The upper arms are part of the back, the hands and the bit belong to the horse. We receive the length of rein that the horse offers. We never take or restrict. The neck is allowed to be at the length the horse requires for balance. When the balance is more advanced, the hind legs will flex more at each joint, the croup will lower and the smooth convex curve of the neck and back will reflect that.

Two to four years on the lunge is the time prescribed for an apprentice in a good riding academy. My sister, growing up in Germany, spent four years on the lunge, as a learner amateur rider. Reiner Klimke, Olympic dressage champion in the 1970s, was lunged once a week all the way through his career. A good seat takes work. How many riders do you know who get worked on the lunge regularly these days? It seems as if we have forgotten the intrinsic value of this basic discipline. Next, we need to gymnasticise our horse's body. The two different sides have to be equalised. Like humans, horses have a stiff side and a supple side. Each side comes with its own dilemma. The over-bent side first needs to be de-contracted to the same length as the long stiff side, then the weight in the footfalls equalised, front to front first then front to back. Then, eventually, the back will take more weight than front not often there often yet. Imagine an Olympic hurdler — the reason they are able to run in a straight line at full speed over obstacles, alternating take off legs, is because the two different sides of their body now work equally efficiently .

The horse's back has to be both strong and supple, the front and back of the horse connected, the neck coming up out of the withers strong and long before it can help lift the back into collection. An educated and fully trained horse should be easy and pleasant to sit on, should move with grace and ease, should float with silent footfalls. Imagine a Victorian lady cruising (sidesaddle, I grant you) in Hyde Park on a sunny Sunday afternoon. That alone could be years of work for the part-time amateur rider with no arena and limited riding time. The traditional school exercises are not just random moves that form part of a competition test. They are all designed to strengthen and supple your horse, to teach better balance, to enable the horse to control his body better and become magnificent. We have forgotten their gymnastic purpose, these strange exercises that appear in our dressage tests. Learning their effects and their criteria takes study — reading, practice, analysis, and educated application. It's not about how they look. It's about how they make the horse feel, how they develop his body, which muscles and joints they target.

Putting the head and neck over a specific hind leg is like power lifting for a horse, developing strength in the haunches. Half passing diagonally across the arena is like the ultimate cross trainer. The half pass is the one of the most spectacular of the advanced movements; the horse moves diagonally across the arena, crossing the legs to achieve the sideways motion. It is also one of the most demanding of exercises, it demands power and strength and suppleness. In practise it develops parts of the horse that other exercises cannot — the reach of the outside hind leg, diagonal power, open shoulders, squats on the inside hind leg when it is done correctly.

Most importantly, you need to win over your horse's mind. They must trust your seat to be stable, trust your hand to be supple yet supportive; they need to reach forward willingly into an allowing contact that offers a point of reference without restricting their balance. The aids are literally signals that assist the horse to find the space he can move into — they offer a point of balance, a frame of reference, not a shoving or a pulling or a pushing that contorts him into a certain shape. The ride becomes a dance, between equal partners.

The horse and human together should become more powerful and more beautiful, and the human will become invisible because it is the horse who should dazzle and shine.

Recommended Reading:

De Kunffy, Charles, *The Ethics and Passions of Dressage*, Xenophon Press (2013)

von Neindorff, Egon, *The Art of Classical Horsemanship*, Cadmos Verlag (2009)

21

IF WISHES WERE HORSES

I f wishes were horses, then beggars would ride.

When I was a child, every single wish I ever made was for a horse of my own. Every shooting star, birthday candle and chicken wishbone prompted a fierce whisper asking for a horse of my own, and on the rare times that I prayed I always made sure to mention my need for a horse (just in case there was a kind deity out there who could dish out real life miracle equines).

I galloped over the horizon every night in my dreams, and all of my playground games involved make-believe horses. I wrote poems about horses, and covered every exercise book with doodles of horses' heads. If wishes were horses, then I would have ridden all day, every day, every single day of my childhood.

I wonder how the books we choose shape our equestrian dreams? I read/devoured/memorised the *Colt from Snowy River* series, the *Black Stallion* series, the *Thunderhead* trilogy, the *Shantih* series. My equine idols all lived out, in fields or on the moors, or on the range, were often ridden bareback, had their natural instincts and characters kept intact, and seemed to have a mystical connection with their special human. I dreamed of jumping, and galloping, fingers wrapped through thick flowing manes with my hair streaming in the wind, communicating by telepathy. I didn't dream of rosettes, of winning or even of competition. I just dreamed of being out with my horses, day after day, enjoying freedom and fun. I did OK. I had some riding lessons aged seven, which stopped pretty quickly once my mum realised that this inconvenient obsession would not be cured by increased exposure. The bus to my all girls secondary school passed an equestrian centre, as well as Mill Hill Boys' School. While my friends were getting off the bus a few stops early to flirt with actual boys, I was racing down to the stables, mucking out in return for the privilege of a fleeting bareback ride while bringing the real, actual horses in from the field. My mum also took me to see the Spanish Riding School in London in the early 80s. In those days, they were still the bastion of correct classical training. The advanced work looked effortless, the horses appeared magical, the synergy between horse and rider invisible.

Years later, when I started competing and having proper lessons, the difference between what I had seen that evening at the Spanish Riding School and what I was being told to do seemed completely incongruous. As a child, I dreamed of dancing with a willing partner, of being able to ride with invisible signals: no force, no pain. I didn't dream of pulling my horse's head in, of making him rounder, of making him submissive. I didn't dream of fighting, or tussling, or arguing with my horse to achieve results. I didn't dream of whipping my horse to achieve an outcome.

Yet that is exactly what we teach kids to do, from a really early age. Any tack shop that caters to children sells lots of pink, spangly, sparkly crops. Some of these may even have decorated stars as the flapper. We call them crops when they are short, for use in general riding or jumping. The longer schooling whips or lunge whips are more honestly named. Lilly, my little neighbour at the previous house, was lucky enough to start her equestrian experience at a local riding school where the children aren't given whips. I was so pleased to hear about a mainstream establishment teaching children the joys of kind communication and ethical horsemanship.

Only last night, Rocky had a meltdown due to a magpie fight in the corner of the arena. After the acrobatics had stopped, we stood, breathed together until his breathing had slowed to normal and his head came down, and then I used grass nuts to achieve willing, self-motivated, forward motion towards the scary corner. The old farmer was passing the arena with the dogs and he laughed at me. He told me I had been watching too many Americans and that I just should get a big stick and teach him what forwards means.

But we did that, last year. And all it got us was grade three ulcers and an even more anxious horse. I don't know if we will be able to fix all of Rocky's physical problems, but when he is calm enough to be able to tell me where the difficulty lies then I might have a chance of choosing the best school exercises to make it feel and work better.

The often quoted eventer's theory that your horse needs to be more scared of you than of the fence is just nonsense. I want my horses to trust me, so that when they see a scary fence they check in, ask if is it OK, and then go for it because I say we can. And, after good training, I want my horses to be so confident that when they see a scary fence it isn't scary because they have seen similar stuff before, been allowed to work it out, and learned that they can do it.

In the long run, I want my horse to be saying, It's OK, I've got this, let's go. We don't get to that point by force, but by education, by life lessons as well as horse lessons. Most of us need life lessons first. And most horse lessons are life lessons, in the end.

I do ride with a whip, but it is a schooling whip, with a leather flapper not a stinger on the end. It's an extension of my hands, for communication, to be able to tap to say this hip, this shoulder, lift your belly or, very occasionally, hey, I'm talking to you. It is never to be used for punishment against the horse. It's a communication device, for very specific aiding moments. *Aider* — verb, French — to help, assist, support, to help to do. That's what the aids should be.

I also do lots of exercises where the whips are used as flags in the hands to show floppy wrists, or held down behind a straight back. My horses tolerate all sorts of whips waving around, because they know the whip won't hurt them, and also because part of the horses' genius is that they really do understand intention. A horse will always know when the whip is something to do with them — pointing at a particular body part during in hand work for example — or when the whip is absolutely nothing to do with them. A whip waved around or flicked in anger will elicit a completely different reaction to a whip waved around with no connection to the horse, or flicked as a signal. If the whip is waved around without intent, it is just background noise, and will be treated as such. Horses absolutely understand intent. And they know when our intent is off target too.

I do jump in spurs, but I was surprised to find that cross country times became much more achievable, not because of spurs or fitness, but because I loosened my legs and learned to balance on my feet in the stirrups and not to grip with my calves. Cal's hind leg could then come forward into the space allowed, his stride got longer and smoother and, hey presto, the magnificent half draught learned to gallop. I also wear spurs for flatwork occasionally, but again they are for refinement. I have done years of work on my legs, with many more years to go, so that I can give an aid for energy with the inside of my foot, not my heel or calf. That means I can use my spurs for specific aids — currently Cal, lift your belly! I am nowhere perfect: our self improvement work as riders is never done, but I can now choose, very consciously, whether I want to use leg or spur.

When I recall my early reading choices, I think it's no surprise that my horses live out as much as possible, mostly unrugged, in a herd, with their key needs catered for. At the last Nelipot Cottage, the horses had six acres and couldn't be described as truly free range, but they had as much freedom and movement and human-free equine time as I could allow them. As well as ample forage, they had an organically managed field with an ever-increasing number of plants, grasses and herbs to choose from, and plenty of life to watch. I'm not trying to tell anyone how they should do things: we all find our own path and our own compromises. And in between physical incarnations of the Nelipot dream, the horses and I are currently back on livery, which inevitably does involve an element of compromise. What I do believe is that we should all continue learning and examine our truths every day of our riding lives.

I vividly remember falling in love with horses, for their noble spirit, and their majesty and their pure grace in motion. When I dreamed of horses, my childhood dreams were full of sound, happy, healthy horses, that were treated as willing partners.

And then somehow, along the way, it becomes OK to hit them with a crop, OK to tie their mouths tight shut, OK to force their heads down, to deny them freedom of expression and to constrain their movements, rather than allow them to show their brilliance, express their opinion or their anxiety.

Did you turn into the owner your horse would dream of? Would your horse pick you? Did your childhood wishes turn into the horses you dreamed of? When you look back to your daydreams, how close you are now to those ideals?

Now that I have learned to listen to my horses, to allow them an opinion and a voice of their own, those make-believe stories, of riding the wind, heart to heart with my dream horse, have become my daily reality.

EPILOGUE

Why did humans start shoeing horses?

This is a question I get asked a lot, and I have been pondering it for it years. There are various horseshoes found in the historical records as far back as 400 BCE. Materials used included plants, rawhide and leather. The Romans write about "hipposandals", and in ancient Asia, there is evidence of shoes made out of woven plants. The application of shoes was not necessarily for protection but also to soothe existing injuries the horse might have sustained in its activities.

At any rate, the practice of horseshoe-making became widespread during 1000 CE, but was limited mostly to Europe. The more nomadic horse peoples, such as the Mongolians, and the Native American Indians, have no history of shoeing their semi-feral horses. My personal premise for the difference between equestrian cultures is that the more industrialised nations moved their horses into cities and walled enclosures with them. When not working, the horses had to be confined to stalls, therefore spending long hours standing in their own urine and pooh. The lack of large scale storage and the need to work hard for long days also meant that the feed provided to the horses had to change — more grain, providing more energy but also more sugar and starch. Gut health would be compromised due to the lack of biodiversity in the diet, and the fact that the horses couldn't forage for 16 hours a day. And their hoof quality would obviously suffer as a result. Which meant these horses couldn't work comfortably with their now compromised hooves. Does this sound familiar?

This is my theory. The semi-feral Mongolian horses I met all had incredibly strong feet, which had never seen a rasp let alone a steel horseshoe, and they do high mileage fast work powered only by the plants they eat along the way and when turned loose in hobbles overnight. They do get fed extra hay in winter when the grass is under snow.

So horseshoes were developed, mostly in Europe where humans first moved into cities and enclosures, to ensure that the domesticated horse can still work hard despite having poor hoof quality due to suboptimal management practice. Now, in our day and age, when horses are leisure animals, kept purely for our pleasure and enjoyment, do we really need to keep our horses in a way that renders them unhealthy? As hooves are the barometer of whole horse health, then a healthy horse should be able to go about their daily business barefoot. If a Przewalski or a zebra was lame in the zoo, there would be uproar. But many people think it is normal for a domesticated horse to be lame without shoes.

Would I ever shoe a horse again? My simple knee jerk answer is no. Not with steel horseshoes anyway. Not now that we have overwhelming evidence that standard steel open heeled horseshoes lead to failure of the crucial structures in the back of the hoof after repetitive shoeing for sustained periods of time. This cause and effect has been well understood since Victorian times.

The only reason I would shoe a horse with steel shoes now is for welfare reasons. And I genuinely can't think of a condition where steel shoes would be the only solution, but

"never is always a lie and always is never true...."

There are great composite plastic shoes available now for rehab purposes, including some really funky work being done on a 3-D printer, literally custom building plastic shoes to order for that horses' specific rehab needs. Most composite shoes last several cycles, so although the purchase cost is high they can be refitted two or three times.

I have never met a horse that couldn't survive barefoot. Survive is a funny word though. Most owners expect their horses to do some work, not simply to be. I have met plenty of owners who thought that their horse couldn't possibly live barefoot, when actually what they mean is that the horse can't yet work at the level required by the human without some foot protection; which for them automatically equates to traditional open heeled steel horse-shoes.

If my horse were unable to do the work I wished her to perform barefoot, I would first ask myself why? I would check the diet. I would improve the environment as much as I could. I would apply all the lessons I have learned, that I am now sharing in this book. I am prepared to take my time and moderate my expectations, and if my horse wasn't ready to go galloping along the stony tracks of North Wales straightaway, then I would buy her a decent pair of hoof boots.

Hoof boot technology has come along in leaps and bounds in recent years. And, unlike the workhorses of old, most modern leisure horses only get used for one or two hours a day. Rather than the horse wearing damaging steel horseshoes for the whole of her life, we can spend five minutes before and after riding putting on hoof boots, that act like sports shoes for horses. Hoof boots enable the horse with less than perfect feet to stride out boldly and confidently on all terrain. Hoof boots allow the hoof to flex as it is meant to, so the horse in boots can strengthen their crucial caudal hoof structures further by moving out well. And the hoof boots can be removed once riding is finished, allowing the horse all the other benefits of committed barefoot hoof care.

Hoof boots are a surprisingly economical solution, as well as being much better for hoof health and horse longevity. The last time I paid to shoe a horse, which was a good few years ago, it cost sixty British pounds for a full set, every five to six weeks. Hoof boots are priced at one to two hundred British pounds a pair, most horses only need them in front, and as I only use mine for extreme hacking, they tend to last for two to three years. If you used them for every ride outside of the arena, I reckon they would still last a year: bargain. Paddy and Rocky have never owned a pair of hoof boots, Cal tried a few brands before we settled on Scoot boots, and after seven years, we are now on our second pair, needed because his feet changed shape. Cal will gallop and jump the small stuff that we encounter out hacking in Scoots. He doesn't need them for jumping on grass so our summer eventing season is fine, and drag hunting in the UK is done in winter mud, when the Cheshire rye-grass is less poisonous and his feet are generally much tougher.

So would I ever shoe a horse again? Not unless I had explored every other avenue. Not with steel, ideally not with nails, and not for my convenience, ambitions or ego. Not everyone of you could make this choice that clearly, and that is fine. I have had to spend many years thinking about this stuff and I have arrived at my level of chosen compromise. And chosen compromises may change, as time goes on and life challenges occur. Your choices will be at a different point on the spectrum to mine, and that is completely fine. As long as we all keep learning, we are all trying to do the best by our horses. The first step is to listen to them, and learn from the feedback. It's a simple credo, but it is not always easy.

ABOUT THE AUTHOR

Fran McNicol is an amateur equestrienne living in the UK. She is a full-time doctor, specialising in surgery. Her MD thesis was an examination of the inflammatory cascade in sepsis.

As a surgeon, MBChB, MD, FRCS, she obviously knows a huge amount about the human animal. But the most useful product of medical training, from her horses' point of view, is that she learned how to research, evaluate evidence and then apply theory to optimise the care of her horses. Her writing is, therefore, a mix of opinion and her current state of learning from 25 years of doctoring, time spent working around the world as a polo groom and many years of keeping her own horses.

Fran loves training young horses and focuses on riding the sport horse both classically and holistically. She competes regularly for her local riding club, especially in One Day Eventing.

Nelipot Cottage started life as an educational blog, to share learning and best practise, to promote the benefits of a barefoot and holistic herd lifestyle for whole horse health, and to reflect on life lessons learned along the way. Fran believes that horses exist to bring out the very best in humans. It is her hope that sharing these tales will bring new friends, kindred spirits, exchange of knowledge and lots of positive energy into the lives of the Nelipot herd.

SEA CROW PRESS

COMMITTED TO BUILDING AN ACCESSIBLE COMMUNITY OF
WRITERS, DEDICATED TO TELLING STORIES THAT MATTER

Sea Crow Press is named for a flock of five talkative crows you can
find anywhere on the beach between Scudder Lane and Bone Hill
Road in Barnstable Village on Cape Cod.

According to Norse legend, one-eyed Odin sent two crows out into
the world so they could return and tell him its stories. If you sit and
listen to the sea crows in Barnstable as they fly and roost and chat-
ter, it's an easy legend to believe.

Sea Crow Press is dedicated to telling stories that matter.

www.seacrowpress.com

Lightning Source UK Ltd.
Milton Keynes UK
UKHW011542011021
391503UK00001B/3